money & morons

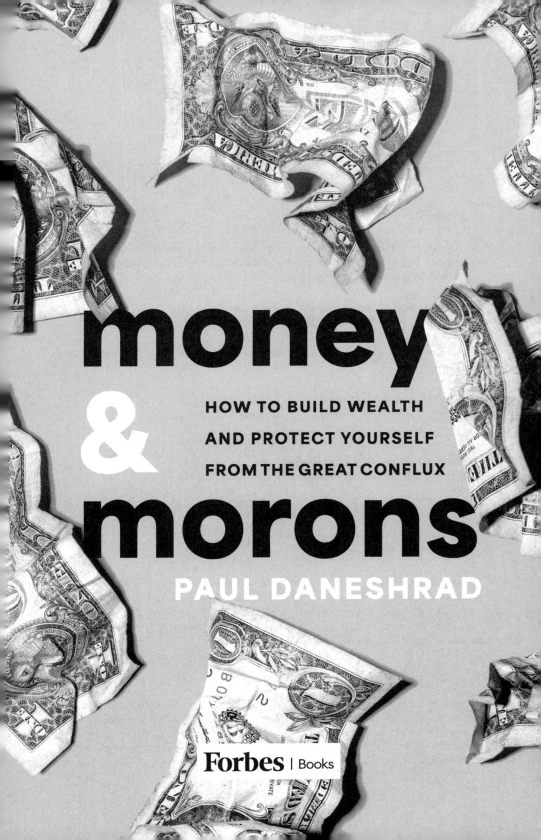

Copyright © 2023 by Paul Daneshrad.

All rights reserved. No part of this book may be used or reproduced in any manner whatsoever without prior written consent of the author, except as provided by the United States of America copyright law.

Published by Forbes Books, Charleston, South Carolina.
An imprint of Advantage Media Group.

Forbes Books is a registered trademark, and the Forbes Books colophon is a trademark of Forbes Media, LLC.

Printed in the United States of America.

10 9 8 7 6 5 4 3 2 1

ISBN: 979-8-88750-076-8 (Hardcover)
ISBN: 979-8-88750-077-5 (eBook)

Library of Congress Control Number: 2023914848

Cover design by Megan Elger.
Layout design by Matthew Morse.

This custom publication is intended to provide accurate information and the opinions of the author in regard to the subject matter covered. It is sold with the understanding that the publisher, Forbes Books, is not engaged in rendering legal, financial, or professional services of any kind. If legal advice or other expert assistance is required, the reader is advised to seek the services of a competent professional.

Since 1917, Forbes has remained steadfast in its mission to serve as the defining voice of entrepreneurial capitalism. Forbes Books, launched in 2016 through a partnership with Advantage Media, furthers that aim by helping business and thought leaders bring their stories, passion, and knowledge to the forefront in custom books. Opinions expressed by Forbes Books authors are their own. To be considered for publication, please visit **books.Forbes.com**.

I dedicate this to my wife, Shadi, and my four children: Talia, Bryce, Bennett, and Ryan. You make me a better husband, dad, and man. I love and adore you all.

contents

about the author... 1
acknowledgments... 3
contact page 5
introduction 7

PART ONE
The Great Conflux: The Obvious and Not So Obvious Reasons Why You Need to Make More Money

1 the growing population: we will all start living much longer 19
2 debts and deficits: a ticking nuclear bomb 43
3 the morons: voters are fueling the fire 71

PART TWO
How You Can Make More Money

4 becoming more productive 99
5 saving: the art of financial discipline 121
6 investing: how to secure your future 137

EPILOGUE
the power of the human spirit and technology............. 161

about the author

Paul Daneshrad is founder and chief executive officer of StarPoint Properties, a private real estate firm founded in 1990. Paul has built StarPoint into one of the most respected real estate investment and development firms in the industry. With over thirty years of experience, and having conducted billions in transactions, Paul is considered an expert in the real estate investment community. He has contributed to many respected publications, including *Forbes, Net Lease Forum, Multi-Family Executive, California Journal of Real Estate, Multi-Housing News, National Real Estate Investor, Real Estate Southern California,* and *Commercial Property News*. Paul graduated from California State University Northridge with a degree in marketing, and lives in Los Angeles with his wife and four children.

acknowledgments

I want to thank my sisters, Sheila and Denise, for their never-ending support. I would not be who I am without your enduring love. A special thanks to Warren Buffett for the decades of advice and wisdom that he has given to all of us who are listening. Thank you, Ryan Dempsey, for making this very challenging book so easy. You are a true professional.

contact page

Paul can be reached by:

Email at AnaL@starpointproperties.com

LinkedIn at Paul Daneshrad

You can follow future dialogue and communications via Instagram at StarpointProperties and Twitter @pauldaneshrad.

introduction

As a kid, I hated when it rained because the roof in our house leaked right onto my bed. I spent many nights on the floor, and when it rained hard enough, leaks kept popping up in different locations, so I'd have to move throughout the night. By the end of a storm, bowls and buckets would be scattered throughout my room to catch all the water.

I grew up in a middle-class neighborhood in Los Angeles, but my parents didn't have the money to properly maintain the home. My mom didn't work, and even though my dad was a professional, he was an immigrant with health issues and a gambling problem, so he struggled to earn a consistent income. He never properly saved or invested his money, so there were many stretches throughout my childhood when there was little to no money coming into the house. Some months, we couldn't pay the electric bill, which meant we'd have to go without hot water or electricity. That never sat well with me, so at the age of seven, I promised myself that I wouldn't live that way when I was older. I definitely knew that my kids weren't going to live that way.

Those early experiences provided me with all the motivation I needed to build a solid financial foundation, so when I was in middle school, I went into business for myself. Remember Bubble Yum? Back in 1982, it had become incredibly popular. Kids were always trading gum and buying single packs. When I saw that the corner store near my house sold packs of five for ten cents, I'd scrape together as much money as possible to buy them up and then sell individual pieces to the kids at school for five cents each.

I learned how to turn a profit at a young age, but bubble gum money only got me so far. When I turned fourteen, I landed my first job at the Hallmark Store, making three dollars an hour after school. I went from there to Carl's Jr. and then Baskin-Robbins. I never made much, but I made sure to save some money. And I didn't stop there.

I wanted to learn as much as I possibly could about money and how to secure my future, so I set out to learn from the best. That's when I discovered Warren Buffett. This was long before he was a household name, but his philosophy resonated with me, so he became a mentor. One thing he said that has stuck with me ever since was to read as much as possible. That's what I did, and by reading I learned about the power of financial independence, compounding, value investing, markets, and, most importantly, diligence and discipline.

By the time I was seventeen, I had a little money saved up, and I used that money to pay for college. I enrolled at California State Northridge and, true to form, had to keep working my way through school, so I got a job waiting tables at California Pizza Kitchen. However, that entrepreneurial spirit was still alive. I used some of the money I made to buy and sell baseball cards, but that wasn't enough to get me through a slow, five-month dry spell at the restaurant. I learned that working for tips as a waiter was a cyclical job. Suddenly, I wasn't making enough to pay for school, rent, and the cost of living. When I came home one day to find an eviction notice on my door, I went to the apartment manager and convinced her to give me a thirty-day extension. Since I wasn't going to spend the little savings I had, I needed to look for a second job.

introduction

Glenfed Development was a full-scale real estate development firm, and even though I knew nothing about real estate, I landed a job being a gofer on weekends. I used my first paycheck to catch up on my rent and vowed that nothing like that would ever happen again.

I had thought about becoming a lawyer in college, but the more I learned about real estate, the more I saw the transformational power of purchasing land and building on it. It was not only a way to make a living, but also a way to build true wealth and financial security. That's what I wanted to do with my life.

Two years after graduating, I accepted a small loan from my sister and brother-in-law, borrowed money on credit cards, and bootstrapped my own business out of my sister's garage. I bought small condos around the city, fixed them up, and flipped them for a profit. I didn't have a strategy at first. I just looked for opportunities where I thought I could make money and pursued them. That was the beginning, and brick by brick, with great diligence and discipline, I built that business into a respected real estate investment and development firm.

Despite what many people believe, the American Dream is alive and well. I'm living proof, but so many fail to achieve their version of the American Dream and get what they want out of life. That trend will only worsen because the playing field is changing rapidly, and those who can't adapt will be left behind because of what I call "the Great Conflux."

> **For the first time in human history, several events are simultaneously unfolding that, when combined, create new levels of risk and contagion not seen before.**

For the first time in human history, several events are simultaneously unfolding that, when combined, create new levels of risk and

9

contagion not seen before. That can be devastating for those who aren't properly prepared. These singular historic events are human longevity, an aging population, and unprecedented levels of debt and deficits.

The first catalyst is the increasing size of the aging population. People are living longer, healthier lives. If you're in your twenties or thirties, there is a good chance you could live to be one hundred or 110. While on the surface that is excellent news, it means that for the first time in history, our nonproductive years will outnumber our productive years. What this also does is put a strain on the government programs designed to support our aging population, specifically Social Security and Medicare. The cost of these programs is one of the main drivers of debt in this country, which has already exceeded $30 trillion. That means we've already passed a 100 percent debt-to-GDP ratio (what we owe compared to what we produce), which is a critical threshold. Very few countries in the history of humanity have come back from that without default or crisis. I believe this risk alone is one of the greatest threats to our future. Let that sink in for a moment, but don't dwell on it for too long because that's only part of the issue.

What makes this problem worse is us, the voting public. We elect people to positions of power who aren't doing anything to address this issue. It's difficult to describe the actions of the American public, our voters, and the Federal Reserve as anything but moronic. This isn't a Republican or Democratic problem—it's a populist problem. Both parties have been egregious with their spending because we keep voting for politicians who don't have the directive or mandate to be fiscally responsible. There are many idealistic politicians who have great intentions and truly care about their constituents and our country. They listen to what their voters want and try to address their concerns. However, our political system doesn't incentivize cutting the federal deficit, reducing expenses, or governing in a fiscally responsible way because those aren't issues that the public prioritizes. Our politicians' first priority is to get elected, and to do that they must deliver what the people want. The problem is that the country can't afford to keep spending and printing money. The path we're on is unsustainable, but if anything is going to change, that directive must come from the voting public. I used to have hope, but when all serious conversations about debts and deficits ended around 2012, I realized that this moronic behavior would continue until we reached a crisis. And we will reach a crisis! When that happens, you need your productive years to be more productive or your quality of life will be in serious jeopardy.

I've been talking to my family and friends about these topics for over a decade. I once brought my distant family into a conference room and presented them with all the data on this subject. I've been a vocal steward of this point to those close to me for years, but until recently, it hadn't gone much beyond that. My goal with this book is to communicate that message to a wider audience and get people to understand, not only the nature of the looming threat, but how to protect themselves and their families.

The good news is that there is time to prepare. None of this will happen immediately. This crisis will most likely come to a head in the next ten to thirty years, but it will happen, and someone will have to pay. The middle class will be the hardest hit, and the average American is not ready. You have a choice to make. You can join the sheep following the moronic voters and leaders hoping they will solve our problems, or you can take control of your own fate and put yourself and your family in the best possible position to thrive.

The path that has allowed me and many other Americans to insulate ourselves involves a basic, three-pronged approach: make more money, save, and invest wisely. Yes, it really is that simple, yet so many people fail to do it.

For one reason, it goes against how we've been programmed as a society. The average citizen knows that a lack of savings is bad, too much debt is dangerous, and the combination of those two can lead to disaster but do nothing about it. Why? One reason is normalcy bias, which is our tendency as human beings to disbelieve or minimize threat warnings. Consequently, individuals underestimate the likelihood of a disaster and its potential adverse effects on them. It's why most Americans aren't concerned about the national debt or their lack of savings.

Normalcy bias may be the reason why so many don't take the impeding threat seriously, but making more money, saving, and investing properly is difficult because it takes time and requires discipline. That's hard, and that lack of discipline is why the average American suffers from the disease of consumerism. Too many people spend money they don't have on material goods they don't need. They also fail to properly save or invest, so it isn't long before they run up their own debt. It's why, according to a July 2021 Bankrate survey, 51 percent of the country has less than three months' worth of expenses covered in emergency savings.[1]

This is the point in the conversation when some begin to push back. "The system is not fair." "I don't have the skills to make more money." "I'm too old to start over." "I have a family to support. I can't save any more money." In other words, people feel stuck and don't see a way out. It's definitely not easy, and I'm certainly not downplaying anyone's struggles, but the reality is that all is not lost.

---

1   Sarah Foster, "Survey: More Than Half of Americans Couldn't Cover Three Months of Expenses with an Emergency Fund," Bankrate, July 21, 2021, https://www.bankrate.com/banking/savings/emergency-savings-survey-july-2021/#:~:text=More%20than%20half%20of%20Americans%20(or%2051%20percent)%20have%20less,from%2021%20percent%20in%202020.

introduction

Warren Buffett said that if you were born in this country, you've won the lottery. What he means by that is you are living in one of the greatest countries on Earth. Fewer than 5 percent of the people in the world get to live here and have the opportunities we have. It doesn't matter if you're an immigrant or a fourth-generation American; you have the opportunity to build a great life for yourself. Opportunity is the key word because nobody is going to give you anything. It starts by changing your behavior and the way you think about money.

Look around your house and see how much crap you've accumulated over the years that you don't need. That's the disease of consumerism at work. Billions and billions of dollars have been invested in advertising that bombards us at every turn and tells us to consume. Everyone is competing for our attention and our dollars. We've been taught and trained to consume, but the grand lifestyle we are being pitched is not attainable for the average citizen without properly saving and investing. Insulating yourself will require hard work, diligence, discipline, and making sound financial decisions. It's not an easy first step to take, but nothing can be improved if that step isn't taken. There is an old proverb that says the journey of a thousand miles starts with the first step. Helping people learn how to take that first step and understanding the implications of the Great Conflux is what this book is all about. That knowledge can help you protect yourself by effectively making more money, saving, and investing.

This book is a wake-up call intended to shed light on our moronic policies and behavior. The title and some of the language I use throughout may be blunt, but I don't want to sugarcoat it because we're harming ourselves, our families, and most importantly, our future. However, you can protect yourself. It doesn't matter your background or age; if you desire to work hard and have the discipline to make money, save, and properly invest, this book can become a valuable tool. But before we can discuss how to become wealthy and stay wealthy, we must first better understand the nature of the threat. In part one, I will go into detail about each of the converging causes of the Great Conflux, starting with the rapidly increasing human life span.

part one

**THE GREAT CONFLUX:
THE OBVIOUS AND NOT SO
OBVIOUS REASONS WHY YOU
NEED TO MAKE MORE MONEY**

CHAPTER 1

the growing population: we will all start living much longer

"Science and technology are the keys to both our longevity and our demise. Our entire existence on this planet is a double-edged sword."

—RHYS DARBY

When the 2020 COVID-19 pandemic hit, my family rode it out like almost everyone else. We hunkered down, kept to ourselves, watched the news, and hoped for the best. I'm a diabetic, so I tried to be extra careful since I was more susceptible than the average person without a preexisting condition. Everything went as well as expected for the first couple of months, but that changed in June.

I went to bed on a Thursday night feeling completely fine, only to wake up Friday morning feeling tired with a few body aches. I felt progressively worse throughout the day, and by Friday night, I had a high fever, trouble breathing, and all the signs of COVID-19. I went to the emergency room at Cedars-Sinai, where I tested positive. They immediately sent me to what felt like the leper ward to spend the night. Sunday morning, my condition had deteriorated to the point where they wanted to put me on a ventilator, but I refused.

I was in horrible shape—so bad that I called up my attorneys and told them to begin preparing my trust. I wasn't sure I was going to make it. The situation had become that dire, and by Saturday night, I was in excruciating pain with a high fever. I was struggling to breathe, let alone talk. The outlook was grim, but I did have one chance, and it was a long shot.

The hospital was participating in a monoclonal antibody trial. As I write this in 2023, this has become part of the standard of care, but back in 2020, there were a lot of unknowns, and the treatment was still in its infancy. I was one of twelve people in the hospital who participated in the double-blind trial, with six people getting the antibody and the other six getting a placebo. That's standard protocol for an FDA trial and a simple way to determine the efficacy of a new drug.

Not only was I not told what I was given, the doctors were also kept in the dark, but anyone who witnessed what happened over the next twenty-four hours did not doubt that I received the drug. I was administered the drug on Saturday night around 8 p.m. By Sunday night, I felt significantly better. I wouldn't say I felt normal, more like I had the flu or a bad cold. Compared to how I felt the night before, I was in great shape. Given how those in the trial responded, it was obvious who received the drug and who received the placebo. My doctors and the infectious disease specialist told me that there was a 90 percent chance that without modern medicine and technology, I would have been a statistic—another victim of COVID-19. Instead, I walked out of the hospital on Monday morning.

My life was saved by modern medicine. I feel lucky to be here, and that experience not only gave me a new outlook on life but also completely changed my perspective. The truth is that it's a great time to be alive. Not just for me, but for all of us. In no other time throughout human history has there been more opportunities available to more people with less of a risk of succumbing to violence, disease, poverty, famine, or death. To many, that sounds ridiculous, but the media has distorted our perceptions. A close look at the facts and data will convince you otherwise.

With the news media trumpeting how horrible everything is, it can be difficult to put the progress we've made as a species into perspective and see how much better life is today for the average person. That doesn't mean everything is perfect. It doesn't mean we should stop trying to improve conditions or solve the real problems that cause people to suffer. But taking the time to reflect on our progress and understand how it was achieved can provide perspective and a road map for the future.

Disease, poor nutrition, poverty, violence, and war impact people at a much lower rate today than they have in the past. Look at famine, or the widespread scarcity of food (which fell to very low levels in the second half of the twentieth century), and you'll see that the last four decades have been particularly low by historical standards.[2] Famine researcher Alex de Waal said that the sharp reduction in famine

---

2 Joe Hasell, "Famine Mortality over the Long Run," Our World in Data, March 22, 2018, https://ourworldindata.org/famine-mortality-over-the-long-run.

mortality rates was one of the great unacknowledged triumphs of our lifetime.[3]

One of the many reasons is the accelerating decline in the world poverty rate. In 1820, the poverty rate was 76 percent. It took 136 years, but by 1956 it dropped below 50 percent.[4] By 2001, that number was cut in half, and in 2022, according to the World Bank, only 8.5 percent of the world's population lives in poverty.[5] Is that still too high? Yes, but that doesn't take away from the remarkable achievement it was to reach that level. We can thank economic growth and widespread access to medicine and food for that. The average American living on an average income today eats better and has more access to food than most medieval kings.

Believe it or not, there is also much less violent conflict that claims significant lives. Pockets of the world remain at war and are stricken by conflict, but war-related death and violence have declined since World War II. In his 2011 book, *The Better Angels of Our Nature: Why Violence Has Declined*, Harvard psychologist Steven Pinker argues that we live in the most peaceful time in human history.

Not only is there evidence that life is more peaceful than ever, but we have more instant access to information than at any time in human history. Using the device you carry around in your pocket everywhere you go, you can look up any fact or piece of information you want. You can get the answer to almost any question in a few

---

[3] Alex de Waal, "The End of Famine? Prospects for the Elimination of Mass Starvation by Political Action," *Political Geography* 62 (2018): 184–95, https://www.sciencedirect.com/science/article/pii/S0962629817302871?via%3Dihub.

[4] Michail Moatsos, "Global Extreme Poverty: Present and Past Since 1820," OECD iLibrary, https://www.oecd-ilibrary.org/sites/e20f2f1a-en/index.html?itemId=/content/component/e20f2f1a-en.

[5] World Bank Group, "Correcting Course," World Bank Open Knowledge Repository, 2022, https://openknowledge.worldbank.org/bitstream/handle/10986/37739/9781464818936.pdf.

seconds and remain in real-time contact with almost anyone around the globe. Tell somebody forty years ago that would one day be possible, and they would think it was science fiction.

Access to information leads to a more educated and intelligent population. Intelligence researcher James Flynn points out how IQ scores need to be recalibrated to match the times. In his 2013 TED Talk, he states, "If you score the people a century ago against modern norms, they would have an average IQ of seventy. If you scored against their norms, we would have an average IQ of 130."[6] That doesn't mean that our ancestors were stupid, but it does indicate that more people have access to the tools necessary to expand our collective intelligence.

> We can live longer, healthier lives, and our children have the chance to live even longer than we might expect.

As impressive as all these achievements are, they still don't match what I believe will be our generation's most significant and impactful advancement (if not a miracle): the increase in our life expectancy. The possibilities are exciting, not only for ourselves and our families but for humanity. We can live longer, healthier lives, and our children have the chance to live even longer than we might expect.

WHAT'S THE NEW LIFE EXPECTANCY?

There is a good chance that you know someone who is more than one hundred years old. That segment of the population has grown by millions worldwide over the past few years. Many are starting to

---

[6] James Flynn. 2013. "Why Our IQ Levels Are Higher Than Our Grandparents." TED video, 18:28. https://www.ted.com/talks/james_flynn_why_our_iq_levels_are_higher_than_our_grandparents?language=en.

live past 110, and while the United States is home to more supercentenarians than any other country, Japan, China, India, and Italy are quickly catching up.[7] By the year 2050, it's expected that there will be 3.7 million people older than one hundred worldwide. That's impressive, considering there were only half a million centenarians in 2015.[8] That's a 700 percent increase in 35 years. So, how long can a human being live?

As of 2022, the oldest person on record lived to be 122. Could that become the norm one day? Could your kids expect to live to that same age? Some experts believe that by the year 2100, it will be possible for the average person to reach 130.[9] A 2020 study using Bayesian population projections estimates the probability that a person will live to at least age 126, 128, or 130 in this century as 89 percent, 44 percent, and 13 percent, respectively.[10] If that ends up being true, it means you wouldn't be considered middle-aged until you're in your sixties.

Some experts argue that the human life span has a ceiling and that we are coming close to reaching that ceiling, but this wouldn't be

---

[7] Renee Stepler, "World's Centenarian Population Projected to Grow Eightfold by 2050," Pew Research Center, April 21, 2016, https://www.pewresearch.org/fact-tank/2016/04/21/worlds-centenarian-population-projected-to-grow-eightfold-by-2050/.

[8] Renee Stepler, "World's Centenarian Population Projected to Grow Eightfold by 2050," Pew Research Center, April 21, 2016, https://www.pewresearch.org/fact-tank/2016/04/21/worlds-centenarian-population-projected-to-grow-eightfold-by-2050/.

[9] Leigh Ann Green, "Maximum Human Life Span Could Reach 130 Years by 2100," *Medical News Today*, July 10, 2021, https://www.medicalnewstoday.com/articles/maximum-human-lifespan-could-reach-130-years-by-the-end-of-this-century.

[10] Michael Pearce and Adrian E. Raftery, "Probabilistic Forecasting of Maximum Human Lifespan by 2100 Using Bayesian Population Projections," *Demographic Research* 44, no. 52 (June 2021): 1271–94, https://www.demographic-research.org/volumes/vol44/52/.

the first time that the ceiling was raised after scientists suggested we had reached a limit. Looking at the average life expectancy throughout history, you'll see that it has steadily increased over time. The ancient Greeks and Romans could expect to live between thirty and thirty-five years. By the mid-1900s, the average human lived to seventy. In 2022, that number rose to seventy-nine.[11]

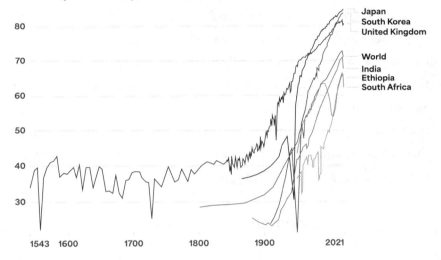

Life Expectancy, 1543 to 2021[12]

It's important to put this in context and understand what goes into configuring life expectancy, which differs from life span. For example, Rome's first emperor, Augustus, lived when the average life span was thirty to thirty-five years, yet he lived to be seventy-five.

---

[11] Liz Stinson, "Our Average Life Expectancy Could Increase to 115 Years Very Soon," *Allure*, August 18, 2020, https://www.allure.com/story/the-future-of-aging?utm_source=onsite-share&utm_medium=email&utm_campaign=onsite-share&utm_brand=allure.

[12] Source: UN WPP (2022); Zijdeman et al. (2015); Riley (2005)
Note: Shown is the "period life expectancy." This is the average number of years a newborn would live if age-specific mortality rates in the current year were to stay the same throughout its life. OurWorldInData.org/life-expectancy.

The reason was that the mortality rate was much higher, especially among the younger population. Today, we suffer from a different type of problem.

Despite the tremendous advancements in modern medicine that have helped prolong the average human life span, it's not all good news. Over the past few decades, the average American life span has only gradually improved. It was seventy-five in 1991 compared to seventy-nine today.[13] It's an increase, but only a small one. While advances in treatment for cancer and cardiovascular disease have taken major steps in the right direction, there has been an increase in the rate of some respiratory, neurological, musculoskeletal, endocrine, nutritional, and metabolic diseases caused by poor diet, lack of exercise, and unhealthy lifestyles that have severely slowed the increase in life span and may even cause it to decrease in some cases. And don't forget that the population is getting older, and aging is the main risk factor for many chronic diseases and disorders.

Average Life Expectancy in the US[14]

---

13   "Cracking Longevity Science," Deloitte, 2022, https://www2.deloitte.com/us/en/pages/life-sciences-and-health-care/articles/longevity-science.html.

14   Source: National Center for Heath Statistics

Many people don't reach the average life span today because of the ailments and vulnerabilities that accompany old age. In 2019, these were the top ten causes of death, accounting for 55 percent of deaths worldwide:[15]

1. Ischemic heart disease
2. Stroke
3. Chronic obstructive pulmonary disease
4. Lower respiratory infections
5. Neonatal conditions
6. Trachea, bronchus, lung cancers
7. Alzheimer's disease and other dementias
8. Diarrheal diseases
9. Diabetes mellitus
10. Kidney diseases

The older we get, the more susceptible we become to these diseases. There is a much higher chance of developing these diseases later in life, which is one of the main reasons for shorter life spans, but there is good news. The reason so many experts predict that the average life expectancy is on the rise is because of a shift in the way we think about and approach healthcare.

Instead of treating the underlying disease, the key to increasing longevity is linked to treating the biological systems that cause aging while promoting wellness and overall healthy lifestyles. That involves targeting cellular senescence and mitochondrial dysfunction. If you slow aging, you limit the number of people who die from age-related diseases and other leading causes of death, thus significantly expanding the life span of the average person.

---

15 "The Top 10 Causes of Death," World Health Organization, December 9, 2020, https://www.who.int/news-room/fact-sheets/detail/the-top-10-causes-of-death.

money & morons

THE RISE OF THE ANTIAGING BUSINESS

Aging is inevitable. It begins in utero, and throughout our lifetimes, various forms of damage and deterioration break down the body and contribute to our overall decline. This has been a battle humanity has waged for as long as we've walked the planet Earth. The quest to live longer is nothing new. Today it's called everything from longevity to antiaging, delaying death, and amortality, but the idea has been pursued for hundreds of years, dating back to the search for the fountain of youth and unlocking the secret to eternal life. The pursuit may not be new, but the demand has never been higher, and that's fueled innovation.

It's not just scientists, researchers, and medical professionals who are interested in increasing the human life span. This burgeoning field has started attracting funding from billionaires, venture capitalists, Silicon Valley start-ups, academic institutions, and governments who have pumped hundreds of millions of dollars into "moonshot medicine" companies that launch research efforts and develop longevity technology.

Fifty longevity companies raised more than $1 billion in venture funding as of 2020.[16] The industry that was worth $54.2 billion in 2019[17] will expand to $64 billion by 2026,[18] and many feel that this

---

16 "Cracking Longevity Science," Deloitte, 2022, https://www2.deloitte.com/us/en/pages/life-sciences-and-health-care/articles/longevity-science.html.

17 Liz Stinson, "Our Average Life Expectancy Could Increase to 115 Years Very Soon," *Allure*, August 18, 2020, https://www.allure.com/story/the-future-of-aging?utm_source=onsite-share&utm_medium=email&utm_campaign=onsite-share&utm_brand=allure.

18 "Anti-Aging Market—Growth, Trends, COVID-19 Impact, and Forecasts (2021–2026)," Research and Markets, July 2021, https://www.researchandmarkets.com/reports/4591836/anti-aging-market-growth-trends-covid-19.

28

is only the beginning. Some predict that funding for the longevity market will outpace existing healthcare along with an overall shift toward wellness and well-being, creating even more opportunities for innovation. Thousands of companies worldwide are working on longevity. To better understand the depth, scale, brains, money, and power behind this human-driven initiative to live as long as we can, here are a few companies leading the charge:

- Altos Labs: Formed by Amazon CEO Jeff Bezos and Russian-Israeli entrepreneur Yuri Milner in September 2021, this company is pioneering new cellular reprogramming technology that will lead to life-extending therapies.
- Juvenescence: Formed in 2016, they have raised over $219 million and are leading the charge when developing prescription drugs and cutting-edge longevity therapies for the consumer health market.
- Insilico Medicine: This company based in Hong Kong was formed in 2014 and has raised over $306 million. They utilize artificial intelligence (AI) to develop and test new prescription drugs for age-related diseases.
- AgeX Therapeutics: Formed in 2017 by biogerontologist Michael West, who has done extensive work in stem cell research and cellular aging, the firm's mission is to reverse the effects of degenerative diseases and aging.
- Human Longevity, Inc.: Peter Diamandis and Craig Venter founded this company in 2013 to use AI, machine learning, and genome sequencing to help treat age-related diseases and reverse the aging process.
- Elevian: In addition to leading the effort to research tissue and organ regeneration, they have developed prescription drugs

designed to fight tissue damage caused by age-related diseases such as stroke and diabetes.

The technology developed by these companies and so many others helps researchers analyze pathology and the causes of some of humanity's most deadly diseases. They work to develop prescription drugs that treat existing diseases and produce therapeutics to prevent disease and reverse the effects of aging by restoring the body's regenerative capabilities. Technology is also one of the main drivers of early detection of chronic illness, which leads to an overall increased life span.

"If we can figure out how to slow aging, we can push out all ten leading causes of death."[19]

—GREG BAILEY, CEO OF JUVENESCENCE

Here are just some of the recent advancements and areas of study responsible for this change in the way we think of healthcare and longevity.

Health Technology

- Lab automation: It sounds simple, but with automation, scientists and researchers can spend less time with tedious lab work and more time applying their skills and expertise to aid research and development. That can lead to the early detection of diseases and the development of new-age drugs. This can increase reliability and improve the overall quality of research.

---

19   Stinson, Liz, "Our Average Life Expectancy Could Increase to 115 Years Very Soon," *Allure*, August 18, 2020. https://www.allure.com/story/the-future-of-aging?utm_source=onsite-share&utm_medium=email&utm_campaign=onsite-share&utm_brand=allure.

- Machine learning: AI's ability to sift through datasets in a fraction of the time it would take a human can ramp up productivity and progress. Machine learning is also used to detect and ultimately prevent disease before diagnosis. AI is quickly becoming a key component in more personalized medicine.
- Wearable devices: The Fitbit and Apple Watch have already become popular among the health-conscious population, but the technology continues to improve. With wearables, you can monitor your heart rate, blood pressure, and sleeping habits, and when used in conjunction with machine learning, the tech can become more individualized to fit your needs. Used properly and consistently, these devices can help improve physical and mental wellness while helping to detect potential health problems before they become serious.
- Nanotechnology: Defined as technology with dimensions less than one hundred nanometers, this is tech so small it can manipulate atoms and molecules. Nanotech can deliver targeted therapies and medications and can also aid in surgery.

Medical Advancements

- mRNA vaccines: The technology has existed for years but made headlines with the creation of the COVID-19 vaccines. What's great about mRNA vaccines is that they cost less to produce and can be developed faster because they don't require the culture of a live virus to manufacture them. In the case of COVID-19, mRNA vaccines have already saved and extended many lives, including my own.
- Senolytic drugs: These are drugs designed specifically to treat senescent cells, which are cells that have permanently stopped

dividing and contribute to age-related diseases such as cancer and cardiovascular disease—two of the world's leading causes of death.
- Therapeutic plasma exchange: This procedure involves removing blood plasma and filtering it through an apheresis machine, where it's reinfused with donated red blood cells and plasma. The procedure has slowed cognitive decline in some patients, while animal studies have shown it to reverse skin, pancreas, muscle, and cardiovascular aging.[20]
- Stem cell therapy: This is a form of regenerative medicine that, instead of relying on full organ transplantation, uses stem cells to regenerate damaged or diseased tissue, reduce inflammation, and improve the function of the immune system. It has been used to treat certain forms of cancer and blood-related diseases, such as leukemia.

In January 2023, Harvard geneticist Dr. David Sinclair and his colleagues published a groundbreaking paper in the scientific journal *Cell* claiming they were able to both speed up and reverse the aging of cells in mice by tweaking the epigenetic information. There was no cell that they couldn't age forward and backward. Human trials are the next step, and Sinclair believes this type of cell rejuvenation has the potential to significantly increase life spans.[21]

---

[20] Aristos Georgiou, "Ninety Will Be the New 40 in 10 Years' Time," *Newsweek*, September 13, 2022, https://www.newsweek.com/ninety-will-new-40-10-years-time-1742152.

[21] Alice Park and Andrew D. Johnson, "Scientists Have Reached a Key Milestone in Learning How to Reverse Aging," *TIME*, January 13, 2023, https://time.com/6246864/reverse-aging-scientists-discover-milestone/.

Areas of Study

- Genomics: This is the study of the human genome and has helped advance the technology around gene editing and disease prevention. Because of technology and research, the cost of genomic sequencing has significantly decreased. In 2012, it cost $10,000, and in 2022, it cost about $600.[22]
- TAME (Targeting Aging with Metformin) Trial: This is the world's first clinical trial on aging. Metformin is a drug used to treat type 2 diabetes, but when researchers learned that those taking the drug had lower mortality rates,[23] they began studying the antiaging qualities of the drug. Metformin is also believed to have significant anticancer properties and can reduce the occurrence of some cancers by 40 to 55 percent.[24]
- CRISPR-Cas9: This technology allows scientists to edit the human genome. Often referred to as "genetic scissors," it involves adding, removing, or altering parts of the DNA sequence. It remains a very new technology, but it shows tremendous promise, which is why in 2020, Emmanuelle Charpentier and Jennifer A. Doudna were awarded the Nobel Prize for its discovery. CRISPR not only has the potential to

---

22 Emily Mullin, "The Era of Fast, Cheap Genome Sequencing Is Here," WIRED, September 29, 2022, https://www.wired.com/story/the-era-of-fast-cheap-genome-sequencing-is-here/#:~:text=Ten%20years%20ago%2C%20it%20cost,Today%2C%20it's%20about%20%24600.

23 C. A. Bannister et al., "Can People with Type 2 Diabetes Live Longer Than Those Without? A Comparison of Mortality in People Initiated with Metformin or Sulphonylurea Monotherapy and Matched, Non-Diabetic Controls," *Diabetes, Obesity and Metabolism* 16, no. 11 (November 2014): 1165–73, https://pubmed.ncbi.nlm.nih.gov/25041462/.

24 "Top 10 Health and Longevity Innovations in 2020," Growing Life, December 18, 2020, https://www.growinglife.com/top-10-health-and-longevity-innovations-in-2020/.

aid in research, but it also means we can rewrite the DNA of animals, plants, and microorganisms, among many other things. It will have a revolutionary impact on our ability to cure genetic diseases.

- Organ rejuvenation: In 2019, Yale University researchers revived a pig's brain after death. Two years later, a kidney was transplanted into a human body from a genetically engineered pig. Scientists are currently refining the process of 3D organ printing to recreate fully functional and healthy organs that can be transplanted into the human body. Much of this technology is in its early stages, but during a time when seventeen people die each day because they aren't able to receive a viable organ transplant,[25] this can save lives and extend the life span of many people.

Right now, many of these options aren't cheap or possible quite yet. There is no getting around the fact that money and poverty play a role in the length of life spans. A 2016 study in the *Journal of the American Medical Association* showed that the difference in life expectancy between the richest 1 percent and the poorest 1 percent was 14.6 years for men and 10.1 years for women.[26] That should be no surprise, given that money makes it easier to live a healthier life and provides more opportunities to indulge in longevity treatments

---

[25] "Organ Donation Statistics," Health Resources and Services Administration, https://www.organdonor.gov/learn/organ-donation-statistics.

[26] R. Chetty et al., "The Association between Income and Life Expectancy in the United States, 2001–2014," *Journal of the American Medical Association* 315, no. 16 (April 2016): 1750–66. Erratum in: *Journal of the American Medical Association* 317, no. 1 (January 2017): 90, https://www.ncbi.nlm.nih.gov/pmc/articles/PMC4866586/#:~:text=First,%20higher%20income%20was%20associated,to%2010.3%20years)%20for%20women.

and drugs. It's been that way throughout history, and the present day is no exception, but the gap is rapidly closing.

As technology increases, the costs of longevity treatments and drugs are expected to decrease. The availability of generic versions of these drugs and the significant increase in the aging population interested in these treatments could help drive down prices and make this option more accessible, but that won't necessarily decrease the margin in life span between the top 1 percent of earners and the bottom. If anything, those margins are only going to increase as our life span continues to increase, thus highlighting the significance of being able to earn more money.

It's not only about living longer—it's also about making those years healthier, and that includes the food we eat. Innovative start-ups focused on improving the quality and availability of food are revolutionizing everything from packaged goods to agriculture. Advancements in robotics have led to innovations in automatic farming that can protect crops, maximize production, and limit harmful pesticides to make our food healthier and the agricultural process better for the environment. And with more companies using technology to expand their commerce platforms, these products have become more accessible to the average person. We continue to have an obesity problem, and many Americans suffer from poor diet and lifestyle choices, but technology is making healthier options more accessible, and never has there been more information and resources available for those who wish to take advantage of them. Many experts feel that it won't be long before annual checkups include more personalized treatments linked to aging.

Whether it's more access to quality food, affordable supplements, state-of-the-art skin-care formulas, or high-tech treatments, these advancements in the longevity space are moving so quickly that many believe that within ten years, people in their nineties could feel like they are in their forties. And it's not only about living longer but about living more healthy, active, and enjoyable lives.

Of course, none of this is written in stone, and there is no way to know if these predictions will be proven right in the coming years. No matter how powerful technology becomes, it can't help us look into the future, but I am certain that for every possible innovation that doesn't materialize, there will be one or two discoveries that far exceed anything we could predict today. That's the beauty of innovation and another reason we live in the best possible time to be alive, but there is a catch. A very big catch.

> **If people aren't financially prepared, life will be challenging at best and catastrophic at worst, making what is possibly a major human achievement morph into what I call "tragic progress."**

The current American economic system, specifically the governmental safety nets and social programs designed to help those over sixty-five, were not designed to support our rapidly growing population. If people aren't financially prepared, life will be challenging at best and catastrophic at worst, making what is possibly a major human achievement morph into what I call "tragic progress." We're already feeling the burden in some areas, and there are two programs in particular that many have come to rely on that *will* soon become insolvent.

THE FUTURE OF MEDICARE AND SOCIAL SECURITY

There is no denying that our aging population is vulnerable, which is why during the Great Depression in 1934, President Franklin Roosevelt announced his intention to create a Social Security program. It was signed into law the following year, and its purpose was to provide social insurance in the form of payments to retired workers over the age of sixty-five, so they could continue receiving income to support themselves. The benefit amount varied depending on how much an individual paid into it (via paycheck deductions) and how much they earned.

The elderly population has the additional burden of added healthcare costs, and many Americans found it difficult to acquire adequate coverage in a market populated by employment-linked group coverage. President Harry Truman first proposed the idea of government-funded health insurance for senior citizens in 1945, but the program did not materialize until 1965, when President Lyndon Johnson signed Medicare into law. It provides health insurance to those sixty-five and older and those receiving Social Security disability benefits.

These are very important programs that were created with the best intentions, but those who designed them couldn't possibly account for how quickly the aging population would grow. Given the post–World War II baby boom, an estimated seventy million people will retire between 2010 and 2030. Ten thousand people will turn sixty-five every day through 2029.[27] This puts a tremendous strain on the Social Security system because there aren't enough workers paying into Social

---

27   Max Roser, Esteban Ortiz-Ospina, and Hannah Ritchie, "Life Expectancy," Our World in Data, October 2019, https://ourworldindata.org/life-expectancy.

Security to support those in need of benefits, but the increase in the aging population isn't the only problem.

When Social Security was created in 1934, the average life expectancy was fifty-nine years. Today that number is seventy-seven, with more and more people living into their nineties and past one hundred. Longer life spans mean higher total payouts, and since wealthier individuals statistically live longer, that further drains the reserves and burdens the system tremendously. The COVID-19 pandemic also hit Social Security hard because the low interest rates prevented those reserve funds from growing. Eventually, something has to give.

The growing elderly population and potential rapid expansion of life expectancy will similarly impact Medicare. The size of the population who qualifies for Medicare is growing faster than the general population. By the mid-2030s, those over the age of sixty will outnumber those under the age of fifteen.[28] According to the MacArthur Research Network on an Aging Society,[29] the population may live between 3.1 and 7.9 years longer than the government projects, creating even further strain than anticipated. This graph from the US Census Bureau shows the projected increase in the sixty-five-and-over population leading up to 2060.

---

28 "Research Predicts Longer Life Expectancy for Americans, Higher Outlays for Medicine and Social Security," MacArthur Foundation, December 14, 2009, https://www.macfound.org/press/press-releases/research-predicts-longer-life-expectancy-for-americans-higher-outlays-for-medicare-and-social-security.

29 "Research Predicts Longer Life Expectancy for Americans, Higher Outlays for Medicine and Social Security," MacArthur Foundation, December 14, 2009, https://www.macfound.org/press/press-releases/research-predicts-longer-life-expectancy-for-americans-higher-outlays-for-medicare-and-social-security.

the growing population: we will all start living much longer

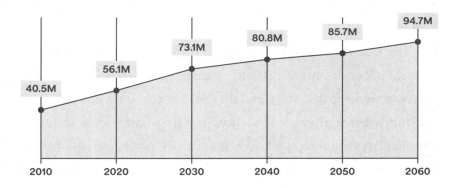

Some projections indicate that the cost of Social Security and Medicare will grow faster than GDP through the mid-2030s because of the aging population, while Medicare will grow faster than the GDP through the late 2070s.[30] Additional taxpayer revenue is required so that these programs can pay recipients, but even that is a temporary solution.

Given the rise in the population and the accelerated cost of living, Social Security and Medicare will be bankrupt shortly. According to the Committee for a Responsible Federal Budget,[31] Social Security will be insolvent in thirteen years, as most trust funds will be depleted by 2035. That means they can't guarantee full benefits to all who qualify, as all beneficiaries will face a 20 percent cut in benefits, but the country's increasing Social Security and Medicare budget is creating a much more dire problem.

With the number of people who the government is committed to supporting through Social Security and Medicare growing, and the time they will need to rely on these programs increasing along with

---

30   "A Summary of the 2022 Annual Reports," Social Security, 2022, https://www.ssa.gov/oact/TRSUM/.

31   "Analysis of the 2022 Social Security Trustees' Report," Committee for a Responsible Federal Budget, July 2, 2022, https://www.crfb.org/papers/analysis-2022-social-security-trustees-report#:~:text=Social%20Security's%20finances%20have%20improved,is%200.12%20percentage%20points%20smaller.

our life span, the Great Conflux is set in motion, but it's only the first domino to fall.

The Congressional Budget Office (CBO) is a nonpartisan government agency whose job it is to create estimates to help the federal government make decisions, and they predict that if we don't fix these two entitlements, they could account for 40 percent of the country's revenue. According to the CBO, mandatory outlays by the federal government totaled $4.8 trillion in 2021. Of that, $1.8 trillion was for Social Security and Medicare.

There is no simple solution to this problem. Some say we need to cut spending, but as soon as you talk about taking away benefits, people's heads begin to explode, and partisan infighting occurs. As Milton Friedman famously said, "Nothing is so permanent as a temporary government program." I understand the dilemma. Nobody wants to vote for or support cuts to essential programs that provide a necessary safety net. The critical problem is that this gargantuan amount of spending puts the country on a path that will likely lead to crisis, thus bringing us to the second converging force at the root of the Great Conflux, the rise of the national debt.

KEY TAKEAWAYS

- Despite what you hear in the media, this is the best time to be alive. Never have famine and poverty been lower worldwide. You are less likely to die due to war or violence, while economic growth has given more people access to food and life-saving medicine than ever before.
- By treating the biological systems that cause aging, the human population will begin to live significantly longer; soon, 130 could become the new one hundred.

- Longevity and antiaging have become a billion-dollar business. This money has been used to create and fund lab automation, AI, wearable devices, nanotechnology, vaccines, plasma exchange, cell therapy, genomics, organ rejuvenation, and CRISPR.
- Poverty plays a role in life span, so the more money you have, the more access you get to higher quality food, treatment, healthcare, and medicine. With the poverty gap rapidly closing and technology bringing down the cost of drugs, a higher percentage of the population will live longer.
- It's not all good news, and there is a significant trade-off that will occur with increased life span. The American economic system and governmental safety programs such as Social Security and Medicare were not designed to support our rapidly growing and aging population. Paying for these programs, and others, will only add to the increasing debt and possibly lead to financial crisis.

CHAPTER 2

debts and deficits: a ticking nuclear bomb

> *"High and rising federal debt makes the economy more vulnerable to rising interest rates and, depending on how that debt is financed, rising inflation. The growing debt burden also raises borrowing costs, slowing the growth of the economy and national income, and it increases the risk of a fiscal crisis or a gradual decline in the value of Treasury securities."*
>
> —THE CONGRESSIONAL BUDGET OFFICE

When I walked out of the hospital after my battle with COVID-19 in June 2020, a friend of mine who is a big philanthropist said, "You have a second chance at life. How are you going to give back?"

Three things immediately came to mind. First, I was going to spend more time with my family. Second, I wanted to be more patient and present. Looking back, I couldn't believe the hours and days I wasted worrying about nonsense, so I made a promise to myself that I wasn't going to sweat the small stuff. It may be a cliché, but that can happen when you come face-to-face with your own mortality. Finally, I wanted to help people. Specifically, I wanted to make an impact in one of the areas I felt was the greatest risk to our country.

It's been three years since my brush with death, and I've maintained my promise to spend more time with my family. That has definitely stuck, but when it comes to worrying about nonsense and sweating the small stuff, I've caught myself slipping back into old routines. I get annoyed over things that I should just let go and allow work and the world to bother me when I know, in the grand scheme of things, it isn't that important. I remain a work in progress, and that endeavor still requires some effort, so I want to make sure I don't give up on that third thing and give back the best way I know how. That starts by discussing a topic I have passionately been sounding the alarm about for over a decade, a topic I believe to be the crux of the Great Conflux: the national debt and deficits.

Ben Franklin said, "Rather go to bed without dinner than to rise in debt." That's a good rule for any individual to live by. It should apply to countries and governments as well, particularly the United States, because it's a rule we have blatantly defied for the past few decades. This will come back to haunt not only us but our children and future generations. The ignorance and endless folly of our voters and leaders who create more and more debt will lead to a crisis, the scale of which the world has never seen, but first we must define our terms.

What is debt? In its simplest form, debt occurs when we spend more money than we make. Most of us know that it's a bad idea to rack up a ton of debt if we don't have the means to pay it back. We all have moments where our spending exceeds our income, and we must put ourselves in check or reap the consequences that come in the form of bankruptcy, failed businesses, and crisis, but not everyone

debts and deficits: a ticking nuclear bomb

realizes that countries can suffer similar consequences if they don't curtail their spending.

A country's income derives from taxes and indirectly through the goods and services that it produces and consumes. The value of those goods and services is referred to as gross domestic product (GDP). The higher a country's GDP and its rate of growth over time is a good indication of a country's economic health. However, too much growth can be unsustainable and lead to inflation. Most economists agree that healthy GDP growth is between 2.5 and 3.5 percent per year. And just like any individual, a country has expenses and must spend money to run its government. In a perfect world, a responsible country would ensure it takes in more money than it spends. When that doesn't happen during a given year, that annual loss is referred to as a deficit.

When a deficit occurs, the government borrows money by selling securities, bonds, and in some cases, printing money to pay for government programs. As a country, the United States has a problem balancing the budget. Over the last fifty years, we've ended the year with a budget surplus only five times. That last occurred in 2002.[32] We've run a yearly deficit ever since, and we aren't even close most years. In 2021, revenues totaled $4.05 trillion, but we spent $6.82 trillion.[33] That is a $2.77 trillion deficit in one year. For some context, the United States did not create $2.7 trillion in debt for over two hundred years combined! Add up all that borrowing year after year, and it becomes the national debt.

So, with that in mind, where do you think the United States stands today? At the end of 2022, the national debt surpassed $31

---

32   "What Is the National Deficit?" Fiscal Data, 2022, https://fiscaldata.treasury.gov/americas-finance-guide/national-deficit/.

33   "What Is the National Debt Today?" Peter G. Peterson Foundation, https://www.pgpf.org/national-debt-clock.

trillion. Let me repeat that: the United States is $31 trillion in debt. In a country of 331 million people, that averages out to about $94,000 per person, but a closer look at the numbers reveals that the problem is even worse than it seems because that figure doesn't account for the unfunded Social Security and Medicare promises. As the chart below shows,[34] the real number is actually closer to $133 trillion if all the off-balance sheet liabilities of the United States federal government are taken into account.

What the Federal Government Has	
Assets	$5.95 trillion
What the Federal Government Owes	
Unfunded Medicare Promises	-$55.12 trillion
Unfunded Social Security Promises	-$41.20 trillion
Publicly Held Debt	-$21.08 trillion
Pension & Retiree Health Care Liabilities	-$9.41 trillion
Other Liabilities	-$2.25 trillion
Total Bills	-$129.06 trillion

Assets - Bills = -$123.11 trillion
Estimated deterioration to date: -$10 trillion

THE TRUTH: -$133 trillion

At least, these were the numbers when I wrote this book. They will have increased by the time this book is published and will have gone up even more by the time you read this.

---

34 "Our Debt Clock," Truth in Accounting, 2022, https://www.truthinaccounting.org/about/our_national_debt?gclid=CjwKCAiAheacBhB8EiwAltVO2za3QD_oSblauOuicm_7mi7E5ad0zmjbmcHbSf18CYjajbRF284BhRoCya0QAvD_BwE.

As incomprehensible as that figure sounds, a country's debt alone is not the problem. Almost every country is in debt, but not all debt is bad, and not all debt is equal. One way you determine when debt is out of control is by looking at a country's debt-to-GDP ratio.

> *"There's nothing inappropriate about having debt in America. It's what helped us grow over time. And it's when debt gets out of control that you worry."*
>
> —WARREN BUFFETT

UNDERSTANDING DEBT-TO-GDP RATIO

A country's debt-to-GDP ratio measures its public debt to its economic output, and it's the best indicator of a nation's economic health.

If we bring it down to an individual level, it's like comparing your income or net worth to your personal debt. That's information banks definitely want to know before they agree to loan you any money because they want to ensure you can pay it back. It works the same way with a country, and the debt-to-GDP ratio is one of the best indicators of a country's ability to pay down its debt.

Accumulate too much debt, and economies not only begin to slow but also suffer.

The higher a country's debt-to-GDP ratio, the greater the risk of defaulting on that debt, but a country doesn't need to default before it suffers the consequences.

Leading economists Carmen Reinhart and Kenneth Rogoff suggest in their industry-changing 2010 economics paper, "Growth in the Time of Debt," that a country with a debt-to-GDP ratio higher than 90 percent will experience a drag on its economy.[35] According to the World Bank, countries with a debt-to-GDP ratio of 77 percent or more for extended periods can experience an economic slowdown, with each additional percentage point of debt costing 0.017 percentage points of annual growth.[36,37] Accumulate too much debt, and economies not only begin to slow but also suffer. When the debt starts taking up more of the GDP, it reduces the GDP, and the economy begins to eat itself. It's a vicious cycle from which few countries can hope to escape.

Every country's situation is different, and there is no universal magic number when it comes to determining the threshold at which a country begins to experience the harmful effects of debts and deficits, but there are some variables to consider. A country's economic output and ability to control its own currency and print money are key determining factors. Wealthy countries can borrow money, while poorer countries find it more challenging. Experts recommend that higher-income countries maintain a debt-to-GDP ratio between 70 percent and 90 percent, European countries between 50 percent and 70 percent, and emerging countries between 30 percent and 50 percent because they have much less margin for error. While every country's

---

35 Philipp Heimberger, "Do Higher Public Debt Ratios Really Reduce Economic Growth?", The Vienna Institute for International Economic Studies, January 18, 2022, https://wiiw.ac.at/do-higher-public-debt-ratios-really-reduce-economic-growth-n-539.html.

36 Raul Amoros, "Visualizing the State of Global Debt, by Country," Visual Capitalist, February 1, 2022, https://www.visualcapitalist.com/global-debt-to-gdp-ratio/.

37 Thomas Grennes, Mehmet Caner, and Fritzi Koehler-Geib, "Finding the Tipping Point—When Sovereign Debt Turns Bad," World Bank Group, June 22, 2013, https://elibrary.worldbank.org/doi/abs/10.1596/1813-9450-5391#:~:text=The%20 estimations%20establish%20a%20threshold,debt%2Dto%2DGDP%20ratio.n.

threshold may differ, responsible debt targets should be fifteen percentage points lower than the country's debt threshold.[38]

Countries can survive and thrive with a high debt-to-GDP ratio, but it can't go on forever. Eventually, the situation will come to a head. When that occurs depends on the country and their situation, but in their book *This Time Is Different: Eight Centuries of Financial Folly*, Reinhart and Rogoff point out that 147 governments have defaulted on their debt (and gone bankrupt) since 1960! They also point out that very few countries have ever returned from a more than 100 percent debt-to-GDP ratio without default or crisis. Unfortunately, the United States has already passed that threshold.

The United States is $31 trillion in debt, but what's even more concerning is that in June 2022, the country's debt-to-GDP ratio was 124 percent. You don't need to be an expert to see that we are on a path to crisis, but before we can discuss a way forward and what this might mean for you and your family, we should dive deeper into the national debt to better understand how this happened.

AN ESSENTIAL Q&A ON THE NATIONAL DEBT

Here is a rundown of some mindboggling debt and deficit figures, current as of January 2023, that everyone should pay attention to:

US National Debt:	$31,477,182,000,000
US Debt per Citizen:	$94,169
US Federal Budget Deficit:	$1,315,032,200,000
US Debt-to-GDP Ratio:	121.51%

---

[38] OECD, "Achieving Prudent Debt Targets Using Fiscal Rules," OECD Economics Department Policy Notes no. 28, July 2015, https://www.oecd.org/economy/Achieving-prudent-debt-targets-using-fiscal-rules-OECD-policy-note-28.pdf.

money & morons

US Total Debt with Unfunded Liabilities $93,641,644,000,000
US Savings per Family $5,074

These aren't static numbers. They are always *increasing*. If you want a good resource for up-to-the-minute numbers on the categories above and more, go to https://www.usdebtclock.org/.

Yes, debts and deficits are complicated. Opinions vary, even among experts, but there are some undeniable facts that can help you better understand the nature of this problem.

How Long Has the United States Been in Debt?

Nothing accumulates more debt than war, and for a country that was founded after a war, it's no surprise that debt has been around for as long as the United States has been a country.

- By 1791, the Revolutionary War put the United States roughly $75 million in debt to the French government and other investors.
- That debt continued to grow, but Andrew Jackson was able to completely pay it off in 1835 by cutting the budget and selling federally owned land. That would be the one and only time in its history that the United States was not in debt. An economic depression occurred soon after, and we never looked back.
- When the country fought the Civil War, the debt skyrocketed from $65 million to $2.7 billion between 1860 and 1865.
- The highest debt-to-GDP ratio occurred during World War II when it hit 119 percent. When the war ended, the economy boomed, and even though the national debt increased, the debt-to-GDP ratio steadily decreased because of inflation and economic output.

debts and deficits: a ticking nuclear bomb

- That decrease continued until 1974, when the ratio hit a new low of 31 percent.
- The debt would fluctuate for a few years before a steady increase began in the 1980s during the Cold War. Except for a few years, it would never slow down.
- The 2008 financial crisis put us on the road toward disaster. We went from a debt-to-GDP ratio of 68 percent in 2008 to a ratio of 82 percent the following year.
- After 2008, spending continued to increase while tax revenue decreased. The US debt-to-GDP ratio surpassed 100 percent in 2013, when the debt was approximately $16.7 trillion.
- The COVID-19 pandemic added insult to injury as federal spending increased 50 percent between 2019 and 2021 due to tax cuts, stimulus packages, and a significant increase in government spending.
- Between March 2020 and June 2022, we added $7 trillion to the debt.

Here is another way to put this into perspective: in 2004, the total debt was only $7 trillion, so in two years, we doubled what it took 215 years to accumulate.[39] The debt-to-GDP ratio jumped from 107 percent in 2019 to 129 percent in 2020, and government spending has only increased since then.[40]

A picture can say a thousand words. The graph below is our debt as of 2022. It will give you the perspective to understand the

---

[39] David Ditch, "These 7 Charts Show Why Congress Must Get Spending Under Control Immediately," The Heritage Foundation, July 7, 2022, https://www.heritage.org/budget-and-spending/commentary/these-7-charts-show-why-congress-must-get-spending-under-control.

[40] Kimberly Amadeo, "US National Debt by Year," The Balance, updated January 18, 2023, https://www.thebalancemoney.com/national-debt-by-year-compared-to-gdp-and-major-events-3306287.

magnitude of the problem and how out of control spending has gotten in recent years. In the 180 years from 1800 to 1980, we accumulated $1 trillion in debt. In the forty years from 1980 to 2020, we accumulated $30 trillion in debt. Yes, $30 trillion! It's worth repeating, and that number is still growing at one of the fastest rates in world history.

US National Debt, 1900-2023

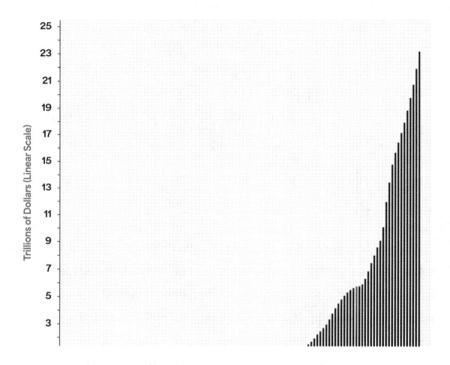

On What Do We Spend Our Money?

These numbers are astronomical, and it can be difficult to wrap your head around how this much spending is even possible, but it raises the obvious question of what all this money is going toward. The federal budget changes every year, and much depends on the administration and its priorities. Let's take 2022 as an example. By September 30,

debts and deficits: a ticking nuclear bomb

2022, $9 trillion had been spent. According to USAspending.gov, this is how the budget for that year breaks down:[41]

- Medicare: $1,484,160,985,812 (16.43%)
- Social Security: $1,296,047,055,351 (14.35%)
- National Defense: $1,181,870,822,425 (13.09%)
- Health: $1,075,778,623,838 (11.91%)
- Income Security: $878,498,463,890 (9.73%)
- Net Interest: $735,945,839,855 (8.15%)
- Education, Training, Employment, and Social Services: $656,975,570,228 (7.27%)
- General Government: $438,617,048,479 (4.86%)
- Transportation: $293,835,384,757 (3.25%)
- Veterans Benefits and Services: $284,351,825,607 (3.15%)
- Unreported Data: $116,242,280,333 (1.29%)
- Community and Regional Development: $103,206,749,197 (1.14%)
- Administration of Justice: $96,289,643,406 (1.07%)
- Natural Resources and Environment: $94,680,950,844 (1.05%)
- International Affairs: $94,557,171,207 (1.05%)
- Commerce and Housing Credit: $72,461,944,828 (0.80%)
- Agriculture: $65,982,456,210 (0.73%)
- General Science, Space, and Technology: $44,721,204,316 (0.50%)
- Energy: $17,785,914,197 (0.20%)

---

41 "FY 2022 Budget," USASpending.gov, 2022, https://www.usaspending.gov/explorer/budget_function.

To Whom Are We in Debt?

This is where things can get complicated, but in its simplest form, debt can be broken down into two categories:

- Intragovernmental holdings: These include debt held by Social Security and Medicare trust funds.
- Debt held by the public: These are treasury securities held by investors. It can include individuals, corporations, the Federal Reserve, and foreign governments. Roughly fifteen countries account for 75 percent of all foreign treasury security holdings, with China and Japan owning the most.[42]

In 2022, $24.35 trillion of the United States debt was held by the public, while $6.89 trillion was from intragovernmental holdings. The debt held by the public has increased by 113 percent since 2012. Intragovernmental holdings have increased by 42 percent since 2012.[43] The reason for the increase is because treasury securities issued by the government are safe, secure, and exempt from state and local taxes, and most can be easily resold on the market. They're also more appealing to the government because the interest rates are lower, which leads us to our next question.

What Does This Debt Cost Us?

What happens when you run up money on your credit card but don't pay the bill in full? You get hit with interest charges on your next bill. The same thing happens with the national debt, which only exacer-

---

[42] "America's Fiscal Future—Federal Debt," US Government Accountability Office, 2022, https://www.gao.gov/americas-fiscal-future/federal-debt.

[43] "America's Fiscal Future—Federal Debt," US Government Accountability Office, 2022, https://www.gao.gov/americas-fiscal-future/federal-debt.

debts and deficits: a ticking nuclear bomb

bates the problem and makes it significantly more difficult to pay it off. The higher the debt, the more government revenue and tax dollars are used to pay it, which limits the government's ability to invest in important public works and services.

According to the Treasury Department figures cited above, the United States devoted 8.15 percent of its 2022 budget to paying $735,945,839,855 in net interest. That is the highest in recorded history, and according to the graph below from the Congressional Budget Office (CBO),[44] those numbers will only increase. Interest costs will grow even faster than Social Security and Medicare, and the CBO expects them to exceed $10 million in the next ten years.

Net Interest Costs Are Projected to Rise Sharply[45]

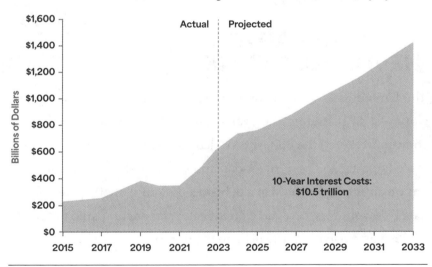

---

44 "The Fiscal & Economic Challenge," Peter G. Peterson Foundation, 2022, https://www.pgpf.org/the-fiscal-and-economic-challenge?utm_campaign=Fiscal%20Challenge%20Funnel&utm_medium=email&_hsmi=170437174&_hsenc=p2ANqtz-_eAEDyl2wctN-7X-MrU2x2jtVfF2wasBmdFDmkhdekg_Bef4HqtGjjmUj6X8ILKUu1BBN_4b3u3lX-qb2YND_p5fAW8rPk6lkdKNW8HdVt52RcmdU&utm_content=170437174&utm_source=hs_automation.

45 Source: Congressional Budget Office, *The Budget and Economic Outlook: 2023 to 2033*, Feb 2023.

Why Aren't Safeguards in Place to Prevent This?

There are! It's called the debt ceiling, and it was created in 1917. It's a limitation imposed by Congress on the federal government to limit the amount of money the United States Treasury can borrow. When that number is reached, Congress must authorize a temporary suspension of the limit, or the government shuts down. You've probably heard talk of government shutdowns every so often. Well, this is the reason why, and it happens frequently. Since 1960, Congress has temporarily raised the debt ceiling seventy-eight different times (forty-nine times during a Republican administration and twenty-nine times during a Democrat administration), but it has never failed to meet its financial obligations.[46] At least, not yet.

A LOOK AHEAD AT THE INEVITABLE FUTURE

The United States may be on the road to crisis, but it certainly isn't alone. Japan is leading the charge. In 2010, Japan became the first country to exceed the 200 percent debt-to-GDP ratio. In 2022, it sits at a whopping 257 percent. Sudan and Greece have since crossed that same exorbitant threshold of a debt-to-GDP ratio of 200 percent. The data below shows where the United States stands compared to the rest of the world regarding the debt-to-GDP ratio.

- Japan: 257%
- Sudan: 210%
- Greece: 207%

---

46   Cecilia Rouse et al., "The Debt Ceiling: An Explainer," The White House, October 6, 2021, https://www.whitehouse.gov/cea/written-materials/2021/10/06/the-debt-ceiling-an-explainer/.

- Eritrea: 175%
- Cape Verde: 161%
- Italy: 159%
- Suriname: 141%
- Barbados: 138%
- Singapore: 138%
- Maldives: 137%
- Mozambique: 134%
- United States: 133%

Japan may not have experienced a crisis yet, but that doesn't mean there haven't been any consequences. During the 1980s, Japan's economy grew significantly, even more so than the United States', but after amassing so much debt in addition to the Bank of Japan raising interest rates to cool down the housing market, it grew stagnant. They experienced virtually no growth between 1991 and 2001. That period is referred to as the "Lost Decade," and they haven't fully recovered. With the rare exception of 2010, when they experienced 4 percent growth, they've been stuck between -1 percent and 2 percent year after year.[47] With such low GDP growth, the debt increased, and with it, the debt-to-GDP ratio.

Despite its stagnation, Japan remains the third-largest economy in the world, but that statistic alone can be deceiving because it was replaced by China as the second-largest economy in 2010. Japan is in such rapid decline that experts project it will be overtaken by India in the next few years and could continue to drop because of an aging population and such a low level of economic growth.[48]

---

47 "Japan GDP 1960–2023," Macrotrends, https://www.macrotrends.net/countries/JPN/japan/gdp-gross-domestic-product.

48 Prableen Bajpai, "The Top 10 Economies in 2027," Nasdaq, December 8, 2022, https://www.nasdaq.com/articles/the-top-10-economies-in-2027.

When you see other countries with higher debt-to-GDP ratios than the United States, it's easy to turn a blind eye and assume that this isn't that big of a deal. However, a closer look at Japan's situation reveals that their extremely high debt level doesn't only impact the government. It also trickles down to impact the citizenry. The chart below shows how the percentage of household savings among Japanese citizens significantly declined along with the rising debt. The huge increase between 2018 and 2020 was due to the government subsidies during the COVID-19 epidemic, which is essentially more debt. The slow growth is actually one of the early signs of a nation burdened by high debt levels and a precursor to crisis or default.

Figure 1: Annual Household Savings Rate[49]

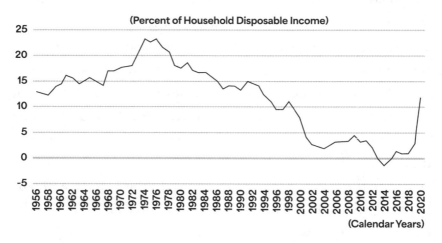

There is a lot we can learn from Japan, but the United States is in a much different, completely unprecedented situation for three reasons.

---

49   Source: Cabinet Office

debts and deficits: a ticking nuclear bomb

1. According to the World Bank,[50] the United States had the world's largest economy in 2021 at $22.9 trillion. China was second at $17.7 trillion, and after that, there was a significant drop-off. Japan was third ($4.9 trillion), Germany was fourth ($4.2 trillion), and the United Kingdom (UK) was fifth ($3.1 trillion). To put the size of the United States' economy in perspective, the state of California on its own would be the fifth-largest economy in the world if it were a country, but that's not the only thing that makes our situation unique.

2. The United States dollar is also the world's reserve currency. That means when the world trades goods, they do so in US dollars. When Saudi Arabia sells oil to Europe, they don't trade in their own currency but in US dollars. The dollar replaced the British pound as the world's reserve currency in 1944 after the UK's exorbitant spending almost bankrupted the country during World War II. To a certain degree, determining the world's reserve currency is a matter of how much confidence you have in that country. If a country can easily be overrun, you don't want to hold on to that country's currency because it could become worthless. Today, you can take your US dollars and go to virtually any port or shop in the world, and they will take that dollar. This is because there is confidence in the stability of the US dollar, and as long as the US dollar is the world's reserve currency, the country can continue to borrow money at a lower cost. But as soon as the world loses confidence in us, we will lose that privilege, and the dollar will lose its value.

---

50 "GDP (current US$)," The World Bank, https://data.worldbank.org/indicator/NY.GDP.MKTP.CD?most_recent_value_desc=true.

3. The United States controls its own currency. That means we can print our own money. Some countries don't control their own currency, which is another factor that causes crises to happen much faster, whereas a country like the United States can keep printing its money to delay a crisis. Some countries peg their currency to the US dollar, so it fluctuates along with the value of the dollar. That means they can't print their own money without experiencing rampant inflation. If that happens, they can't offload their currency because nobody wants to buy it. It's very hard to print money when you peg it to another currency. And when other countries experience economic distress, they want our dollars and bonds. When the world uses those, it creates an incentive for us to print more money.

Those three factors give the United States a lot of ability to increase the national debt and will allow us to keep kicking the can down the road ... for a little while, at least. Eventually, that runway will end. When that happens, nobody will want to hold on to our currency or our debt. It's hard to predict when we might lose that trust, but given the way we're going, it's only a matter of time.

In the 1970s, 1980s, and 1990s, it would have been possible to work ourselves out of debt, but after the 2008 financial crisis and the 2020 COVID-19 pandemic, the country started printing so much money that we passed the point where we are realistically capable of pulling ourselves out of debt. That leaves us with two options: default or crisis. What does that mean? Let's take a look at default first.

While one country could default at a debt-to-GDP ratio of 80 percent, another might not default until they reach a debt-to-GDP ratio of 180 percent. It completely depends on the economic structures of the country. Given the amount of runway the United

States has, it's unlikely we will default, but we remain in completely uncharted territory.

That leaves the most likely option: crisis. That can result in any number of disasters. One scenario is that we inflate the debt away just by continuing to print money. That most likely won't happen all at once or be as sudden as the 2008 financial crisis. This crisis will evolve slowly. We'll have a little less money, and everything will cost a little more. Eventually, the social fabric will begin to unwind.

The correlation between printing money and inflation is direct, and examples of this date back hundreds of years. It's the reason why people have sought gold, and today, it's that same theory behind Bitcoin. The voting populace—and, in turn, governments—act irresponsibly when it comes to their currency, and despite the recent devaluation of cryptocurrency, the argument in favor of a currency like Bitcoin is that it is finite. The government can't print more Bitcoin or devalue it by making more. This is not an argument for or against Bitcoin, but simply an observation.

Another possible outcome is social unrest. This happened in Germany after World War I. When the country experienced massive debts and economic turmoil from rampant inflation due to money printing, someone came along and convinced the populace that he could solve all their problems. That man was Adolf Hitler. That's an extreme outcome, but it's an example of what kind of crisis can result from economic instability.

HOW THIS WILL IMPACT YOU

No matter what form it takes, this crisis won't only impact the United States; it will be felt globally. First, anyone holding our dollars or debts will flood the market trying to sell, and a collapse will occur, similar to a run on a bank. That could force the entire world into a recession, but it's impossible to predict what might happen and when because we find ourselves in an unprecedented situation. No country like the United States, with this amount of runway, has ever been in this situation before, but that doesn't mean we won't feel the impact. Listed below are some impacts of debts and deficits.

Decreased Economic Growth

Debt is a growth killer. Sustained or increasing levels of debt will undermine the country's ability to invest in its economy, which slows down economic growth. One common element among the countries with the highest debt-to-GDP ratios is that they have low-growth economies.

Currency Depreciation

If the dollar depreciates, imported goods become more expensive, and the country can become less competitive on the global stage.

Financial Instability

High levels of national debt can create instability in the markets, impacting stocks, bonds, and commodities. That creates uncertainty, which leads to higher volatility in asset prices, and a greater likelihood of financial crisis.

Political Instability

High levels of national debt create tension and can result in government policies meant to alleviate the concerns of the people, even if they aren't in the country's best interest. This can create more debt and further economic challenges. In some of the worst cases, it's led a country into regional conflict and sometimes war.

Decreased Trade

High levels of debt can make our trading partners lose confidence in us, making us less competitive in the global market. It can lead to a reduction in exports and can create trade imbalances, which can reduce GDP and result in a further reduction of economic growth.

Basic Governmental Function

Aside from reduced financial and fiscal options, countries forced to carry high levels of debt find it difficult to properly allocate their resources. With so much money going toward the debt, that means money can't be spent productively on investment, infrastructure, and defense.

National Security Concerns

> **High levels of national debt create tension and can result in government policies meant to alleviate the concerns of the people, even if they aren't in the country's best interest.**

The higher a country's debt-to-GDP ratio, the riskier it is to loan that country money. Much like what happened with the United Kingdom, if it ever appears that the United States can't protect our allies or ourselves during wartime, we risk losing our status as a global superpower. The harsh reality is that rising interest rates will increase the national debt and make it more difficult for the country to secure more funds during times of national crisis. Remember that the debt-to-GDP ratio was only

68 percent going into the 2008 financial crisis. If something similar occurred today with our current debt, it would be much more difficult for us to rebound.

However, it's not just the government but the country as a whole that suffers. It's so easy to read this and feel like this problem has nothing to do with you, but a drag on the economy can impact individuals in a myriad of ways. And it doesn't happen all at once. It can feel like death from a thousand cuts, but here is a rundown of how you and your family might begin to feel the effects of the growing national debt.

Inflation

This one is a no-brainer. Whether groceries cost more or the price of gas increases, you will first begin to feel the impact in your pocketbook. When the country borrows more money, American businesses might appear to be riskier investments, which forces them to raise prices so they can pay off their own debts. Everything gets more expensive, and that reduces your purchasing power while eating into your savings and decreasing your overall wealth. Inflation is an absolute killer to an economy, and it also does extraordinary damage to the lower and middle class.

Rising Interest Rates

When the Federal Reserve wants to stimulate the economy, they lower interest rates, but they can't do that anymore because debts and deficits are so high. When they want to slow an economy to prevent inflation, they raise interest rates, which can make housing unaffordable, increase credit card debt, and mean that you pay more interest on your loans.

debts and deficits: a ticking nuclear bomb

In 2022, the Fed increased interest rates. They are trying to create a soft landing but are more likely to put us into a recession. This is contrary to the very purpose of the Federal Reserve, which is to keep us on the road to stability, but they have no choice. Believe it or not, inflation is a greater threat than a recession. Federal Reserve Chairman Jerome Powell made combating inflation a priority because he knows it will be "painful," but compared to inflation, a recession is the lesser of two evils.[51]

Lower Home Prices

When buyers can't afford homes at the listing price, those prices will decrease over time. This might sound good to potential buyers, but if you're already a homeowner, it might decrease the value of your property. Others believe that inflationary forces may counteract this deflationary force.

Higher Taxes

When debt and spending increase, taxes will be raised, not just for the wealthy, but raised for everyone. This will result in less income for the average individual, which makes it harder to save and invest. The rich and mobile can move to countries with lower taxes. Even those who choose to remain or are looking to invest will do so in countries with less tax burden, so they can keep more of what they earn.

---

[51] Lodewick, Colin, "Jerome Powell says the Fed is ready to 'bring some pain' to households and businesses. 'These are the unfortunate costs of reducing inflation,'" *Fortune*, August 26, 2022. https://fortune.com/2022/08/26/jerome-powell-fed-inflation-recession-pain-jackson-hole/.

Decreased Income Leads to Decreased Savings

When the government borrows money, it creates a counterproductive cycle that can negatively impact people and businesses alike. When corporations are taxed at a higher rate, that forces companies to decrease their investment, which leads to a decrease in productivity and profits. It also means a decrease in income for employees. Lower employee wages result in decreased savings.

Government Benefits Decrease

Every dollar the government spends paying off the growing debt, and the growing interest on that debt, is a dollar it can't spend on programs such as healthcare and education. That has a very real impact on you and your family.

> *"I have long argued that paying down the national debt is beneficial for the economy: it keeps interest rates lower than they otherwise would be and frees savings to finance increases in the capital stock, thereby boosting productivity and real incomes."*
>
> —ALAN GREENSPAN, FORMER CHAIRMAN
> OF THE FEDERAL RESERVE

* * *

There is no one-size-fits-all policy or approach that every country can take to reduce debts and deficits, but we can't rely on growth alone. On average, our growth rate is roughly 3 percent. Our most productive years are offset by recession years, but over time we can rely on the GDP being around 3 percent. At that rate, growth will never outpace debt at the rate the country currently accumulates debt.

debts and deficits: a ticking nuclear bomb

Some people think you can tax your way out of this problem, but to do that, we'd have to significantly increase taxes, not just on the rich, but on everyone. As former President Ronald Reagan said, "We don't have a trillion-dollar debt because we haven't taxed enough; we have a trillion-dollar debt because we spend too much."

This is not conjecture or bias. There is significant research to support this. A 2022 Tax Foundation study found that "a one percentage point cut in the APITR (average personal income tax rate) resulted in an immediate increase in GDP per capita of 1.4 percent and by up to 1.8 percent after three quarters."[52] Raising income taxes will almost always negatively impact GDP. Raising taxes also negatively impacts the amount of money people can invest, while cuts to the marginal tax rate correlate with a decrease in the unemployment rate. That means it's easier to find a job when taxes are lower, and those jobs are likely to pay more because a decrease in taxes leads to an increase in wages.

Politicians and the public are hesitant to cut entitlement programs, and I understand why, but a 2018 study[53] revealed that those cuts would be less harmful to growth when compared to tax increases. Spending cuts are shown to be a much more effective method of reducing the debt-to-GDP ratio. This doesn't mean that we should never raise taxes because it can create growth and stability. Tax increases must be part of the solution. I know that I should pay more in taxes, but we can't solve this problem by only raising taxes. Not only will it be ineffective, but the wealthiest Americans will move

---

52   Vermeer, Timothy, "The Impact of Individual Income Tax Changes on Economic Growth," *Tax Foundation*, June 14, 2022. https://taxfoundation.org/income-taxes-affect-economy/#:~:text=*A%201%20percentage%20point%20cut,in%20GDP%20after%20three%20quarters.

53   Alberto Alesina, Carlo A. Favero, Francesco Giavazzi, "Climbing Out of Debt," *Finance & Development*, March 2018. https://www.imf.org/Publications/fandd/issues/2018/03/alesina.

their money and invest elsewhere. Hard working and highly talented people will leave, and there will be nobody to replace them. However, the bigger issue is that we won't even get close to chipping away at the massive numbers we're talking about through taxes alone, so that's not a realistic solution either, at least not by itself.

Any solution that doesn't begin by cutting spending is not a solution that will be effective. If we want to dig ourselves out of this hole, we must tighten our belts. There is no way around that. We must cut spending to allow our GDP to grow at a higher rate than our debt. If we can grow GDP at 3 percent and the debt only grows at 1 percent, the problem will be solved in thirty or forty years, but that also comes at a cost. Spending cuts can reduce GDP and have a significant impact on those who require government support.

The reality is that this problem has become so big and complex that there is no single solution that will prevent hardship or pain, but hardship and pain is a better option than the crisis we will inevitably experience if we continue on this path. Since nobody wants to make a sacrifice, we're at an impasse and can't come up with a solution. If that weren't bad enough news, there is one more wrinkle that makes such a significant change seem unlikely, and it's the next phase of the Great Conflux.

KEY TAKEAWAYS

- The United States is $31 trillion in debt—$133 trillion if you consider unfunded Social Security and Medicare promises.
- A country's debt-to-GDP ratio is the best indication of its economic health. Economic slowdown occurs at 77 percent. A drag on the economy begins at 90 percent. Very few countries have ever come back from a debt-to-GDP ratio of 100 percent

without defaulting or experiencing an economic crisis. The United States is at 124 percent.
- The United States is in a different situation and has a much longer runway before reaching crisis because we are the world's leading economy. The US dollar is also the world's reserve currency, and we print our own money, which buys us some time but doesn't solve our problems.
- This crisis won't occur all at once but could slowly result in decreased economic growth, the depreciation of the dollar, financial instability, political instability, national security concerns, inflation, rising interest rates, higher taxes, higher home prices, decreased income, and fewer government benefits.
- We can't increase GDP to cover the cost of our debt, and we can't tax our way out of this problem. The only viable solution is to curb spending.

CHAPTER 3

the morons: voters are fueling the fire

> *"To preserve our independence, we must not let our rulers load us with perpetual debt. We must make our election between economy and liberty or profusion and servitude."*
>
> —THOMAS JEFFERSON

Steve Jobs changed the world.

The iPhone alone completely transformed how we live by providing access to an almost unlimited amount of information through a device we carry around in our pockets. Despite his achievements in consumer technology and communication, not to mention what he accomplished after purchasing Pixar and through his environmental and philanthropic endeavors, Jobs was not without his flaws. He may have been brilliant, but he was human, so he was not exempt from making moronic decisions.

In 2003, Jobs underwent a CT scan to look for kidney stones, but his doctors discovered something much worse. The shadow they saw on his pancreas turned out to be cancer. Cancer is terrifying, and pancreatic cancer is even more terrifying because it is one of the deadliest forms of cancer. However, Jobs was lucky. The cancer detected was a neuroendocrine islet tumor, which is a much rarer and slow-growing tumor that comprises only 5 percent of pancreatic cancerous tumors. That makes it the most likely type of pancreatic cancer to be cured through surgery, but Jobs didn't undergo surgery—at least not right away.

Instead, Jobs opted to undergo alternative and experimental treatments that involved dietary supplementation, fruit juices, and acupuncture. This was a guy who had grown so used to going against the grain, doing things his way, and taking chances that he didn't think twice about thwarting conventional medical wisdom, much to the chagrin of his family, friends, and doctors. But this was one risk that didn't pan out. The alternative treatment didn't work, and finally, Jobs decided to undergo surgery, but nine months had passed since he was diagnosed, and the cancer had spread. Although he survived for eight more years, he lost the opportunity to get out in front of this vicious disease, and it cost him his life.

Walter Isaacson worked with Steve Jobs in his final years to craft his biography and revealed that Jobs later regretted his decision to forgo surgery for so long. He was a brilliant man whose unique vision changed how we live and communicate, yet he couldn't see what was so obvious to everyone else. It doesn't matter how smart you are. We are all human, and human beings are prone to moronic behavior from time to time, so we can all do stupid things.

If there is one important lesson to learn from Steve Jobs's story, it's that you shouldn't take risks that have catastrophic consequences. Even if the risks seem remote or distant, or even if there is only a 1 percent chance, do everything in your power to avoid that risk. Everything! Yet this is something we instinctively don't do. And unfortunately, it's something the people who are in charge and running our government today definitely don't do. Take one look at some of the policies being promoted by politicians and that becomes abundantly clear.

MORONIC POLICY ON DISPLAY

During times of crisis, the United States government has an obligation to step up and help its people. We can disagree on where to draw the line between what is necessary and what is fiscally irresponsible, but I've lost hope that our voters and politicians can make that distinction. There is no better example of this than the COVID-19 stimulus payments.

> We can disagree on where to draw the line between what is necessary and what is fiscally irresponsible, but I've lost hope that our voters and politicians can make that distinction.

When the world shut down in March 2020, a significant portion of the American public could not work. People were confined to their homes, which meant that many middle- and low-income households felt the squeeze. Over the next two years, two different administrations would pump money into the economy to help ease the people's burden until life could return to normal. Between March 2020 and March 2022, borrowing increased by over $6 trillion.[54] While the inten-

---

54 "How Are We Paying for the Federal Response to the Coronavirus?" Peter G. Peterson Foundation, March 15, 2022, https://www.pgpf.org/blog/2022/03/what-role-has-federal-debt-played-in-the-response-to-the-covid-19-pandemic#:~:text=Since%20March%201%2C%202020%2C%20Treasury,legislation%20to%20date%2C%20was%20enacted.

tions behind the relief effort may have been good, and the idea had merit, there is no denying that the execution was botched.

Did you realize that many millionaires and even a handful of billionaires received stimulus checks?[55] They didn't do anything illegal or wrong. They followed the rules and they fit the criteria to receive relief as laid out by the federal government. These were people who owned businesses, created and maintained jobs, and followed program guidelines. Some businesses really needed the stimulus, but the number of businesses that did not yet receive payments is staggering.

GoDaddy CEO Bob Parsons is a billionaire who received an $8 million Paycheck Protection Program (PPP) loan during the pandemic to help support his sixteen businesses, but instead of taking the money, he gave it back because he felt other businesses needed it more.[56] Even though his businesses were losing money during the pandemic, he could easily weather the storm, and he was right, but the decision to give back a government handout is one that very few people would make. Most of those who received money from the government kept it, whether they needed it or not, and there's nothing wrong with that because it's within their right to do so. The problem is that too many people received stimulus payments who didn't need them, and the dramatic increase in the savings rate during the pandemic proves it.

According to the Federal Reserve, the savings rate in the United States soared to record-high levels during the pandemic. Our collec-

---

55   Picchi, Aimee, "At least 18 billionaires got federal stimulus checks, report says," *CBS News*, November 5, 2021. https://www.cbsnews.com/news/stimulus-check-18-billionaires-relief-payments/#:~:text=Included%20among%20the%20billionaires%20who,%243.7%20billion%2C%20the%20report%20noted.

56   Kristin Stoller, "Why GoDaddy Billionaire Bob Parsons Gave Back His $8 Million PPP Loan," *Forbes*, https://www.forbes.com/sites/kristinstoller/2020/05/14/why-godaddy-billionaire-bob-parsons-gave-back-his-8-million-ppp-loan/?sh=194ae87f592e.

the morons: voters are fueling the fire

tive bank account savings grew from $800 billion to $5 trillion in less than thirty-six months.[57] The chart below paints a powerful picture.[58]

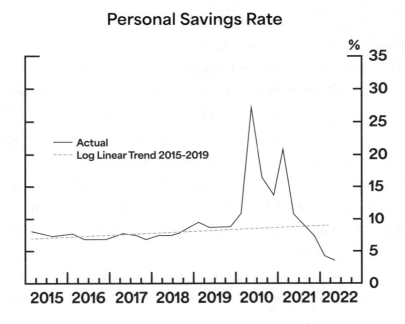

Many people did need assistance, but those aren't the only people who received money. There were many individuals and businesses who received government assistance even though they would have been perfectly fine without it. I don't blame them; I blame the system. Why else would the savings rate spike during a global pandemic (while most of the people in the country were under quarantine) if the people receiving the money didn't need it? If everyone needed the money, it wouldn't go directly into their savings. Government stimulus and

---

57   CRE Analyst, "10 Headlines You'll See in 2023," LinkedIn, December 14, 2022, https://www.linkedin.com/pulse/10-headlines-youll-see-2023-cre-analyst/.

58   Aditya Aladangady et al., "Excess Savings during the COVID-19 Pandemic," Board of Governors of the Federal Reserve System, October 21, 2022, https://www.federalreserve.gov/econres/notes/feds-notes/excess-savings-during-the-covid-19-pandemic-20221021.html.

distress funding should never add to the savings rate, especially when it's adding to the debt and deficit, but that's not all that money was used for.

According to a 2022 Consumer Finance Protection Bureau (CFPB) report,[59] many of those stimulus recipients who weren't padding their savings accounts were paying off their credit card debt. The report shows a sudden decrease in credit card debt from March to June 2020, and then again after the Economic Impact Payments in January and March 2021. However, it's clear that nothing was learned, and any relief was short-lived, because a majority of those individuals and households found themselves back to the same level of pre-pandemic debt by February 2022 and once again struggling to pay bills. In general, these COVID-19 stimulus payments were a miscalculation, an inefficient use of capital, and just another example of moronic policy.

All this money had to come from somewhere, so the government just printed more. And as Reinhard and Rogoff pointed out, printing money leads to inflation, which is exactly what happened in 2022 when inflation reached a forty-year high.[60] And for what? How much of that money was essential and used for its intended purpose? As time passes, more and more stories emerge about hundreds of billions of dollars in

---

59 Erik Sherman, "Household Financial Health Is on the Decline, Says CFBP," Globest. com, December 22, 2022, https://www.globest.com/sbm-gbst/2022/12/22/household-financial-health-is-on-the-decline-says-cfpb/?kw=Household%20Financial%20Health%20Is%20on%20the%20Decline%2C%20Says%20CFPB&utm_source=email&utm_medium=enl&utm_campaign=multifamilyalert&utm_content=20221222&utm_term=rem.

60 Kimberly Amadeo, "US Inflation Rate by Year from 1929 to 2023," *The Balance*, December 14, 2022, https://www.thebalancemoney.com/u-s-inflation-rate-history-by-year-and-forecast-3306093.

relief money that was improperly allocated or stolen,[61] but this isn't the only example of moronic policy and government inefficiency.

Healthcare makes up a significant percentage of our current debt, and it's only going to increase in years to come due to the increasing aging population and human longevity. According to the Organization for Economic Co-operation and Development (OECD) chart below,[62] as of July 2022, we already spend significantly more on healthcare per person than most of the industrialized world.

If the amount we're spending isn't bad enough, we're also not getting the quality of care we're paying for. According to the Common-Wealth Fund, the United States ranks last, out of eleven high-income-

---

61 Eamon Javers and Scott Zamost, "Criminals Have Stolen Nearly $100 Billion in Covid Relief Funds, Secret Service Says," CNBC, December 21, 2021, https://www.cnbc.com/2021/12/21/criminals-have-stolen-nearly-100-billion-in-covid-relief-funds-secret-service.html.

62 "What Is the National Debt Today?" Peter G. Peterson Foundation, https://www.pgpf.org/national-debt-clock.

producing countries that were studied for quality of healthcare.[63] We spend the most, by far, and have the lowest grade in overall quality.

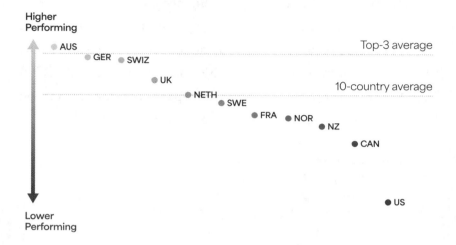

Given how much a program like Medicare has grown, and how much money the federal government has devoted to it, fraud has become rampant. The government can't afford to conduct proper oversight, so the system is easily manipulated by patients and doctors alike to their advantage. I've witnessed it with my own eyes. Our current system has created an incentive to bill Medicare for unnecessary or extra treatment that ultimately ends up being paid by the taxpayers. This is exacerbated because the government doesn't conduct any means of testing, meaning that they have no way of knowing whether a millionaire who doesn't need Medicare still receives benefits. Social Security suffers from a similar problem. I've paid into it for my entire working life, much more than the average person, but even

---

63 Eric C. Schneider, Arnav Shah, Michelle M. Doty, Roosa Tikkanen, Katherine Fields, Reginald D. Williams II, "Mirror, Mirror 2021: Reflecting Poorly – Health Care in the U.S. Compared to Other High-Income Countries," *The Commonwealth Fund*, August 4, 2021. https://www.commonwealthfund.org/publications/fund-reports/2021/aug/mirror-mirror-2021-reflecting-poorly .

though I don't need it now, I will still get it. That's moronic policy and part of why we're in this mess.

The government is too large to run a tight ship, and if they did pay people to try and catch all these little indiscretions, the cost would probably be higher than what they could legally recover. All of this is a clear indication that despite the good intentions of both these programs, they have extended beyond the scope of what the government is capable of doing.

I've experienced something similar with my own company. When we opened our doors in 1992, we were a tiny organization with two employees literally working out of my sister's garage. It may not have seemed like it at the time, but running the business was much simpler back then. When we started to grow in size, I faced new problems every step of the way. Now that we have hundreds of employees (which is still a small organization in comparison to some of the larger companies), I've been forced to deal with issues that are more complex and harder to control. The same is true for the US government, but they have an even bigger problem that makes it more difficult for them to right the ship.

It's hard to control everything, but as a business owner, I have incentives that the government does not have. If I waste a dollar, I will feel the impact, but if I find a way to save that dollar, I can put it back into my business. It's the same when keeping track of any family or individual budget. You feel immediate benefit or punishment based on your spending habits.

The federal government doesn't work the same way, and those who run these programs have no personal or immediate incentive to cut costs. If they waste a dollar, there are no immediate repercussions; if they save a dollar, it doesn't go back to them. That leads to inefficiency and a lack of alignment. It's just human nature, making it difficult to care about the bigger picture. This creates a level of inefficiency, waste, and added expense that we as a country can no longer afford.

One reason we aren't getting what we pay for is because the government has grown to the point where it's taking on some roles it wasn't designed for. Without significant changes to the programs and sources of funding, both Social Security and Medicare are going to run out of money, and anyone who argues with that is doing so in bad faith. None of this is news. Many have seen the writing on the wall for a while now, but the longer we wait, the more costly the potential adjustments and the fewer available policy options. Rising debt levels and time close the door on gradual change that would allow people to adjust. Proposals have been made, but the government and our elected officials have not taken action to fix the problems with either of these programs. The path we're on now with these two government programs is unsustainable. Meanwhile, we keep printing money and getting further and further into debt as a country.

POLITICS MAKES EVERYTHING WORSE

Before we get into this topic, I will state up front that this is not a political book that attempts to point the finger at one party or the other. It's the populace who is at fault. That means us, all of us. Republicans, Independents, and Democrats are equally to blame. This is not a partisan issue. This is a political and populist issue, and a very complex one with no easy solution anymore.

When it comes to spending, Democrats and Republicans share the responsibility. When the debt-to-GDP ratio was at an all-time high during World War II, Harry Truman (Democrat) was president. Richard Nixon (Republican) was in office in 1974 when the debt was

the morons: voters are fueling the fire

at an all-time low. Ronald Reagan (Republican) spent a lot on national defense during the Cold War in the 1980s. While Jimmy Carter and Bill Clinton (both Democrats) served, the debt-to-GDP ratio did not steadily increase. The chart below gives you an indication of how both major political parties have impacted our debt levels, but keep in mind that there are always extraneous circumstances, such as the Financial Crisis and the COVID-19 pandemic that can impact spending.

US Gross Federal Debt by President

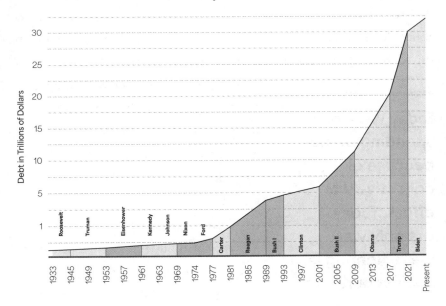

Politicians were able to curtail spending and bring down the national debt after World War II, but the political landscape and how we talk about spending have completely changed. Everyone could get on board with government spending when the fate of the free world was on the line during World War II. Politicians were much more conscious about the debt, but today we aren't spending money because of a collective war effort. Today the only war we're fighting is against ourselves.

Leaders from both parties have spoken out about the need to control our national debt and cut spending. Democrat Barack Obama said, "Increasing America's debt weakens us domestically and internationally. Leadership means that 'the buck stops here.' Instead, Washington is shifting the burden of bad choices today onto the backs of our children and grandchildren. America has a debt problem and a failure of leadership."

Republican Senator Mitch McConnell has made similar comments about debts and deficits: "Put simply: if we do nothing to pay down this debt and address the needs of Social Security, Medicare, and Medicaid, then America risks finding itself so weakened financially that someday in the not-too-distant future, we just won't have the resources we need to equip and maintain our forces in the places they're needed most."

> Today we aren't spending money because of a collective war effort. Today the only war we're fighting is against ourselves.

Political partisanship and polarization are at an all-time high. Each party believes the other is a threat to democracy, and they aren't shy about vocalizing those opinions, because it's what their most ardent supporters and voters want to hear. The media stokes the flames, and we're bombarded with messaging about how the stakes couldn't be higher with each election. It's gone beyond hyperbole, and each administration appears to believe it because once they get into office, they try to get as much done as possible in the shortest amount of time—as if they feel they will never be in power again. That results in astronomical spending. The paradox is that it's all our fault. We are the first ones to blame. We are letting it happen because we have the power the vote, to decide what our priorities are and who we place in governmental positions of power.

Excessive government spending has become the new norm. Fiscal responsibility has gone out the window. Most politicians no longer have a serious conversation about debts and deficits because any attempt to provide solutions to this complex problem could negatively impact their electability. I don't blame them. They listen to their constituents and need to get elected to make an impact. When confronted with debts and deficits, even many of the so-called experts provide excuses, or worse, insist there isn't a problem at all. There is one emerging and truly moronic trend that, if it catches on, could be especially dangerous.

THE ABSURDITY OF MODERN MONETARY THEORY

The diagnosis is clear, but our condition as a country is not yet terminal.

We know what will eventually happen if we continue to spend money we don't have, and we know the national debt continues to increase, but we still have time to fix this problem. We've done it before, and there are ways for us to do it again. It will take sacrifice, and it will be painful, but it can be done. However, like Steve Jobs, we aren't taking the logical route. There are even a handful of economists who put their faith in the economic equivalent of Steve Jobs's herbal remedy: Modern Monetary Theory (MMT).

Investopedia defines MMT as "a macroeconomic theory that says that countries that control their own currencies, like the United States, are not constrained by revenues when it comes to government spending."[64] In other words, since they have a monopoly on issuing their currency, they are different from individuals and businesses that must be constrained by a budget, and it's the reason why government policy should not be influenced by rising debts and deficits. Proponents feel that government agencies will solve our problems.

That sounds great on paper, but is there any evidence that shows something like this could work? No. None. If anything, historical data shows the complete opposite, that prolonged debt forces countries into crisis. Yet some voters and economists quote MMT to justify why we no longer have to worry about debts and deficits.

Just because there may not be any direct constraints of a country's national debt on its economy doesn't mean there aren't indirect constraints. There are always economic constraints. An economy can't consume and invest more than it produces and imports for extended periods of time. The ability to print money doesn't change this. The reality is that too much debt slows down economic growth, so spending must be reduced in certain sectors of the economy to rebalance the debt-to-GDP ratio.[65]

Even if you don't buy into that thinking, another reason MMT is moronic goes back to what I call "the nuclear theory." If there's even a 5 percent chance that your country might find itself involved in a cataclysmic event, like nuclear war, you do everything possible as a leader to avoid that outcome. You don't take that risk because the stakes are too high. If you're wrong, the outcome would be devastating. Even a 1 percent chance of catastrophe is too much of a risk. The

---

64 Deborah D'Souza, "Modern Monetary Theory (MMT): Definition, History, and Principles," Investopedia, April 12, 2022, https://www.investopedia.com/modern-monetary-theory-mmt-4588060.

65 Michael Pettis, "How Does Excessive Debt Hurt an Economy?", Carnegie Endowment for International Peace, February 8, 2022, https://carnegieendowment.org/chinafinancialmarkets/86397.

national debt works the same way. You don't want to put the world at risk by piling on debt when you have no evidence or data to support a theory, and that's exactly what it is: a theory! Yet that's the risk the proponents of MMT are willing to take.

Buying into theories like MMT can be disastrous and essentially blow up the entire economy, but we've seen smart people make moronic choices throughout human history. Sometimes smart people can be convinced by people they trust to buy into moronic theories. This is especially true when those theories provide a convenient solution that prevents us from resorting to an uncomfortable alternative solution. That's why MMT remains a discussion point and hasn't been put on a level akin to voodoo. The government and the voters aren't coming to save anyone.

HOW MUCH OF THIS IS OUR OWN FAULT?

When it comes to debts and deficits, what's the difference between the United States and China, or a democracy and communism?

If living in a communist state where the leaders accumulate debt and the people don't have influence, except to take up arms, they can blame leadership. When living in a democracy, the people have a fundamental tool in the ability to vote that allows them to change the direction of leadership. If the people choose not to use that tool because of self-interest and comfort, they can't blame leadership. They have the power to vote for leaders who can make debts and deficits their primary goal. With enough of those people in leadership, there will be change, but that won't happen until the people are willing to sacrifice. That's why I can't sit here and put the blame on the politicians' shoulders.

It's easy to complain about leadership and make them the scapegoat, but politicians pay attention to what they need to, so they can serve and get elected. No politician today can talk about debts and deficits and expect to get elected. That's why you don't see any debt hawks running for Congress. The incentive structure in American politics is to do the opposite and promise solutions and handouts, even if they aren't practical and put us further into debt as a country. Democracy fails when you reach the point where the public can't identify catastrophic risk and continue to vote for policies that increase that risk. That's where we're at, and for that, I blame us.

The politicians may not have the directive to make debts and deficits a priority, but the populace has become too lazy and conflicted to vote for fiscal responsibility. Instead, they want an easy fix. For some, the need for government assistance is real, and that segment of the population shouldn't vote for cuts or increased taxes. We must continue to support that constituency, but there are a growing number of people who don't require the federal safety net yet still expect someone to swoop in and solve their problems. Until those people can stop spending, become financially disciplined, and learn how to save and invest, nothing will change. That's why we as a citizenry shoulder most of this blame.

When news spreads about government incentives, entitlements, and stimulus payments, people are on board because they assume that it's free money. It's not, but as long as the people don't educate themselves about the issues, the problem with our debts and deficits will only worsen.

Cutting the national debt will require making tough decisions, taking away luxuries, and getting back to our high productivity levels. The bottom line is that people don't want to do that, and politicians know they can't get people to vote for them when discussing that

the morons: voters are fueling the fire

strategy. They can't tell people they will cut benefits and spending in their jurisdiction and expect to win elections. There is no political incentive to tackle this issue, so they ignore it, even if they know it will have catastrophic consequences in the future. If you pulled most politicians aside and got them to talk off the record, I'm fairly certain they would admit that the national debt is a major problem. There is just no way you can get most of them to say it publicly, and I don't blame them.

The point being made in these three chapters isn't controversial. You don't have to look at these figures very long to see that something's incredibly wrong, and most people know that. If you ask people if the growing national debt is a problem, most will say yes. They may not understand the severity of the problem if they don't follow the issue, but it's one that almost everyone can acknowledge. According to the Peter G. Peterson Foundation's Fiscal Confidence Index, in March 2022, 83 percent of voters said their concern about the debt increased in recent years, and 76 percent wanted the rising national debt to become a top political priority.[66]

We have to recognize and appreciate the paradox. The people know it's a problem. They just don't want it to be their problem, and they won't vote for the politicians who want to cut entitlements, raise taxes, or reduce the deficit. They want it fixed, but without any pain and not on their dime. Not only is this an excellent example of cognitive dissonance, it also introduces normalcy bias—which is the natural human reaction to underestimate the potential damage of an event or set of circumstances by pretending the problem doesn't exist—into the equation. Normalcy bias goes well beyond wishful

---

66 "US Fiscal Confidence Near Record Low as Nation Enters Era of Rising Interest Rates and Economic Uncertainty," Peter G. Peterson Foundation, March 31, 2022, https://www.pgpf.org/press-release/2022/03/fci-press-release?utm_source=dcm&utm_medium=link&utm_campaign=baf.

thinking and is much closer to denial. Part of the human paradox is that our typical reaction to an uncomfortable feeling or issue is to escape that feeling as quickly as possible. The human brain will seek out a solution to discomfort or dissonance, even if that solution is misaligned with our goals and intentions and might even do us harm in the future. This has become the standard reaction for politicians and citizens alike regarding the topics that comprise the Great Conflux.

It's easy to assume that because a disaster like this hasn't occurred yet and we've been fine so far, things will continue to be fine. How many disasters throughout recent history (be it World War II, COVID-19, or the financial crisis) turned out to be much worse than anticipated because we did not initially recognize the severity of the problem? It's amazing how, as humans, we can naturally tune out or downplay the truth if it's not immediately convenient; especially when a catastrophic risk appears to be in the distant future. It's easier to avoid pain and difficult decisions now. Ignorance can be bliss ... at least for a little while, until a disaster occurs and we aren't prepared.

ACCEPTING REALITY

Can we solve this problem? Yes. Will we? No way in hell! The reason I'm being so blunt is to make the point that the problem has become so big and so complex that we as a nation must accept that there are no easy solutions. Until voters and politicians make this issue a priority, crisis will most likely occur, and I'm not the only one who thinks like that.

The CBO (the nonpartisan government agency whose job it is to create estimates that help the federal government make decisions) doesn't see a solution on the horizon. In fact, their predictions show our debts and deficits steadily increasing. According to the graph

the morons: voters are fueling the fire

below, we will hit a debt-to-GDP ratio of 200 percent within a generation. Remember that the CBO is a non-partisan arm of the government meant to provide information and data-driven projections.

Public Debt at Highest Since 1946[67]

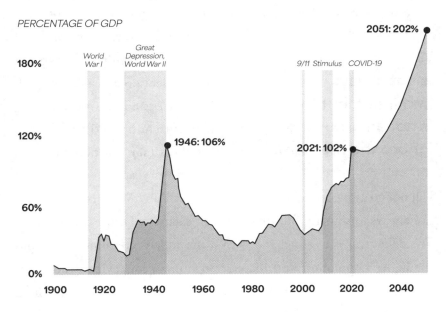

These predictions could be considered modest because they don't consider recessions or financial disasters. Every seven or so years, there is a dip in GDP. Go back a hundred years, and you will see this same trend. It's impossible to predict when the next financial crisis, pandemic, or recession will hit, but we can be certain it will occur, and that could very easily catapult us toward crisis sooner. Fitch, one of the world's leading rating agencies, recently reduced the country's credit rating citing a concern over the country's direction and debt levels. One of Fitch's primary objectives is to evaluate and identify risks.

---

67   Source: CBO, Heritage.org

Karen Dynan, an economics professor at Harvard, senior fellow at the Peterson Institute for International Economics, and former chief economist at the US Department of the Treasury said, "Such a high level of government debt would impair economic growth by crowding out private investment, constrain the government's ability to respond to future adverse developments, and put the country at risk of fiscal crisis. Policymakers will therefore need to take action in coming years to put government debt on a sustainable path by raising taxes and cutting spending relative to current projections."[68]

> **What is inevitable is not always imminent, but that is not an excuse to ignore the problem.**

The crisis may not occur for ten, twenty, or thirty years, but this problem will not go away. Somebody will have to pay for it. What is inevitable is not always imminent, but that is not an excuse to ignore the problem. The debt crisis is coming, and with it the added economic stress from the aging population and increase in human longevity—the Great Conflux. The harsh reality is that when it does, the burden will fall on your shoulders. You will be responsible for the financial stability of you and your family, and just because we are living longer doesn't mean we have more time to generate income. It might be painful and require sacrifice at first, but I promise that it will be worth it in the long run.

"Hard times create strong men, strong men create good times, good times create weak men, and weak men create hard times."

—G. MICHAEL HOPF

---

[68] Karen Dynan, "High Inflation and Fiscal Policy," Peter G. Peterson Foundation, 2022, https://www.pgpf.org/expert-views/inflation-interest-and-the-national-debt/high-inflation-and-fiscal-policy.

OUR PRODUCTIVE VERSUS NONPRODUCTIVE YEARS

We are not only living longer as a species, but we have the opportunity to live healthier lives. With all this talk of ninety being the new forty, we have the chance to look and feel great. We can do a lot more beyond the age of sixty-five than we ever thought possible fifty years ago, but that doesn't mean we're going to see an increase in our productive years.

Our mental capacity significantly drops off in our late fifties and early sixties. We're past what I call our highly productive income-producing years (HIPY), which are the years between twenty and fifty-five when we're at our peak and can produce and perform at a high level, both physically and mentally. Many people can work past the age of sixty-five, but they are not in their prime. Talk to those in their sixties or seventies about having to put in a full twelve-hour workday, and it's much more challenging than it would be for those in their forties. Those years are what I call our nonproductive income-producing years (NIPY). They are the years when we're past our prime, not generating much income or tax revenue, and drawing on the country's reserve resources, particularly Social Security and Medicare.

Even though it's illegal, there are stats that show most employers really don't want to hire anyone past the age of fifty-five. Once you get to about forty-nine, your ability to get hired for a long-term position diminishes substantially, never mind being hired for a critical, high-paying job. It's even harder when you reach your fifties, and forget about your sixties. That doesn't mean people don't get hired at that age, but the fact that it's uncommon is no secret.

The chart below shows how as our longevity increases, our NIPY, or retirement years, will outpace our HIPY, or the years when we are best prepared to earn money. It's the first time in human history that will occur.

Period	Starting Age of HIPY	End Age of HIPY	Avg. Life Expectancy	# of HIPY	# of Non-Productive Income Years (NIPY)
1700s	15	30	30	15	0
1800s	15	35	35	20	0
1900-1950	20	55	60	35	5
2000s	20	55	75	35	20
2050 (proj.)	20	55	90	35	35
2070 (proj.)	20	55	100	35	45
2100 (proj.)	20	55	124	35	69

Previous generations had twenty years to work, save, and invest for five to twenty years of retirement. Future generations will have twenty years to work, save, and invest for thirty-five to sixty-nine years of retirement.

As this mega trend continues to grow, and we have the same number of HIPY to support the ever-growing number of NIPY, we must make sure that our HIPY are more productive. But is this something future generations are prepared for? A 2022 Northwestern Mutual survey[69] revealed that members of Gen Z plan to retire at age fifty-nine, which is twelve fewer years than the baby boomers. It's an ambitious goal, considering this generation will have the longest NIPY period of any previous generation.

---

69 "America's Youngest Adults Plan to Retire Earlier Than Any Generation Before Them," Northwestern Mutual, December 19, 2022, https://news.northwesternmutual.com/2022-12-19-Americas-Youngest-Adults-Plan-to-Retire-Earlier-Than-Any-Generation-Before-Them.

With the proper preparation, it is possible to thrive. There is so much to live for. I would love to be a teenager today and know that I could live to be 110 or even older. But for those who aren't prepared, this is the worst possible time to have a higher percentage of the population living deep into their NIPY, because who wants to be 110 and broke?

As a result of the Great Conflux, the reality is that the system can no longer support you if you can't support yourself. You have a choice to make. There is still time, but you must act now to insulate yourself, especially the younger generations who are likely to live past the age of one hundred. What follows in part two is a blueprint for how to do exactly that!

KEY TAKEAWAYS

- The COVID-19 stimulus payments are one example of moronic policy on display, as large swaths of Americans who didn't need the money received checks.
- The United States spends significantly more on healthcare per person than any other country in the industrialized world, and those costs will only rise with the growing population and increasing human longevity. As Medicare has grown, so has fraud—and lost taxpayer dollars with it.
- The government has grown to the point where it's exceeded the scope of what it was designed to do. Worse, the incentives aren't there for leaders to right the ship. This leads to waste, inefficiency, and added expense.
- We all, Independents, Democrats, and Republicans, share the blame for excessive government spending, as politicians need a clear mandate to make this a priority. If they talked about

reducing spending and decreasing the debt, they would never get elected.

- According to Modern Monetary Theory, countries that control their own currency are not impacted by debt and government spending. No evidence exists to show that this would work, and all historical data points to the opposite. A country can't spend more than it produces and expect to survive. The ability to print its own money doesn't change this.
- We the citizens need to accept the blame as well, because we vote the politicians into power. Too many people want a quick fix or for the government to swoop in and save them, but that will never happen.
- Normalcy bias is our natural human reaction to underestimate the potential damage of an event or set of circumstances by pretending the problem doesn't exist. This is exactly what we and our politicians have succumbed to regarding the debt.
- The CBO predicts that we will reach a debt-to-GDP ratio of 200 percent within a generation.
- Because we are living longer, we need to make our productive years more productive. We used to have twenty years to work, save, and invest for twenty years of retirement. Future generations will have twenty years to work, save, and invest for thirty-five to sixty-nine years of retirement.

part two

HOW YOU CAN MAKE MORE MONEY

CHAPTER 4

becoming more productive

"Labor passes quickly, but the fruit of labor endures."

–MUSONIUS RUFUS

"It must be so nice to have a rich family, so you could inherit your money. Do you ever feel guilty for not having to work for your success?"

That's what Peter, a recent business associate, said to me while out to dinner with me and my wife. He was talking about how there was less competition to make money in the '80s and how he was glad that his kids would have it easy as well. My wife glanced at me several times because what Peter was saying couldn't have been further from the truth.

Peter wasn't familiar with me or my history, but this wasn't the first time someone had said something like this to me. What I find so interesting about these interactions is that many people assume that those who are wealthy had it easy and didn't have to work hard to earn their money. That couldn't be further from the truth. In fact, the data indicates the opposite.

Living in the United States, we have advantages that many people around the world don't. I've talked about a few of them already. The United States is the world's largest economy. We have the highest GDP and GDP per capita in the world. The dollar is the world's reserve currency. Our democracy is stable (for now), and we have become a haven for capital. And because of capitalism and democracy, we are a global tech and business powerhouse, attracting some of the best minds and business leaders from all over the globe. The clock may be ticking, but for now, there is opportunity to be had.

Believe it or not, you have an easier chance of becoming successful while living in the United States than in any other country. That's why the United States is home to more new millionaires than anywhere else. We have only 4 percent of the world's population, but 40 percent of the world's millionaires. That's twenty-two million out of the fifty-six million total millionaires worldwide. The next closest country is China, with five million millionaires. In 2020, we added 1.7 million new millionaires alone, and they didn't all achieve that status through inherited wealth. Of those new millionaires, 79 percent didn't receive an inheritance.[70] I know this is possible. I was a waiter at CPK making $12,000 a year and now I'm in the 1 percent of earners in the United States; part of the 56 million millionaires and part of an even harder-working group of Americans who achieved this while growing up in poverty. The opportunity is there, but you wouldn't realize it by looking at what's happening to the middle class.

---

70 Abby McCain, "33 Incredible Millionaire Statistics [2023]: 8.8% of US Adults Are Millionaires," Zippia, February 24, 2023, https://www.zippia.com/advice/millionaire-statistics/.

The United States once had one of the wealthiest and most prosperous middle classes in the history of the world, but that middle class is quickly dying. According to wage statistics released by the Social Security Administration, 50 percent of all American workers made less than $3,133 a month. That's $37,596 a year before taxes.[71] When the average rent for a single-family home in 2022 was $2,495 a month (up 13.4 percent from 2021),[72] not much is left to live on. Wages may be increasing, but according to a 2022 report, they aren't outpacing the inflation rate.[73] Considering the inflation rate reached 8.5 percent in October 2022, it could be considered the biggest pay cut in twenty-five years.[74]

The other 50 percent of the population isn't doing much better. The Social Security Administration report stated that 30 percent of Americans made less than $20,000, 41 percent made less than $30,000, 52 percent made less than $40,000, and 62 percent made less than $50,000. Thirty years ago, these statistics might not have been a problem. People could live a comfortable life on much less, but inflation, money printing, apathy, and moronic policy decisions by our voters and elected leaders have significantly changed the standard

---

[71] "Wage Statistics for 2021," Social Security Administration, https://www.ssa.gov/cgi-bin/netcomp.cgi?year=2021.

[72] Kate Dore, "Rent Prices Are Soaring in These 5 US Metros. Here's What to Know Before Moving to a Cheaper Area," CNBC, August 2, 2022, https://www.cnbc.com/2022/08/02/rent-prices-are-soaring-in-these-5-metros-what-to-know-before-moving-.html.

[73] Jon Hilsenrath and Rachel Wolfe, "People Have Money but Feel Glum—What Does That Mean for the Economy?" *Wall Street Journal*, July 14, 2022, https://www.wsj.com/articles/people-have-money-but-feel-glumwhat-does-that-mean-for-economy-11657808195.

[74] Robert Rich, Joseph Tracy, and Mason Krohn, "More Workers Find Their Wages Falling Even Further Behind Inflation," Federal Reserve Bank of Dallas, October 4, 2022, https://www.dallasfed.org/research/economics/2022/1004.

of living while eroding the middle class and decreasing their purchasing power.

The bottom line: Too many Americans struggle to get by and live paycheck to paycheck, preventing them from securing their future. But if we are the wealthiest country in the world with so many advantages, how did we get ourselves into this situation?

ATTITUDES HAVE CHANGED

According to the U.S. Bureau of Labor Statistics, the labor productivity rate has dropped from a high of 2.8% annual growth between 1947 and 1973 to a low of approximately 1.5% between 2007 and 2022.[75] Experts believe that higher productivity rates could add $10 trillion to GDP, but without a massive increase in technology, productivity is unlikely to return to previous levels, and there is a chance that an increase in technology could come at the expense of available jobs.

This decline in productivity is true for businesses and it's true for individuals. Jobs are available. In fact, during and after COVID-19, even industrial firms offered signing bonuses for jobs that require little to no training or education. That was unheard of before, but it's indicative of the struggle some sectors are experiencing to fill positions. Why is that?

The new reality is that a certain portion of the population simply doesn't want to work low-paying jobs or has realized they can get by through handouts, entitlements, or other forms of government assistance, such as unemployment. When people see that they can

---

75 Charles Atkins, Asutosh Padhi, and Olivia White, "What the most productive companies do differently," *McKinsey Global Institute*, February 16, 2023. https://www.mckinsey.com/mgi/overview/in-the-news/what-the-most-productive-companies-do-differently .

becoming more productive

make almost as much money from unemployment and other sources as they can from working, they decide to accept unemployment. They aren't all lazy. Some are trying to bide their time until something better comes along. Others are frustrated and not engaged. Others lack training. There is no easy solution, and these trends can differ among sectors, but one thing is clear: government handouts to those who don't require a handout need to stop. However, that's only half of the problem.

Outside of those suffering from homelessness, drug abuse, and mental illness, I believe this problem can partially and directly trace back to a lack of motivation, work ethic, and discipline. There is no better example of this than the moronic phenomenon of Quiet Quitting.

Quiet Quitting has gained popularity on social media, particularly with Gen Z. It means not going above and beyond at work. It means doing the bare minimum to keep your job. It means not looking out for your fellow employees or the company. This short-term thinking results in doing as little as possible. Sure, some people have always done this in some form, but it's becoming more popular in recent years. According to a 2022 Gallup survey,[76] 54 percent of the workforce born after 1989 falls into this category. It's no surprise that this portion of the workforce is the first to complain that their future is not secure, they have no savings, they are being left behind, capitalism doesn't work, socialism is better, and the system is rigged. There is no end to the excuses.

---

[76] Lindsay Ellis and Angela Yang, "If Your Co-Workers Are 'Quiet Quitting,' Here's What That Means," *Wall Street Journal*, August 12, 2022, https://www.wsj.com/articles/if-your-gen-z-co-workers-are-quiet-quitting-heres-what-that-means-11660260608?gclid=EAIaIQobChMIucCkh7iz-wIVhNqGCh11HAQoEAAYASAAEgKuf_D_BwE&mod=&psid=WSJ_DSA_GOO_ACQ_NA&gclsrc=aw.ds&ef_id=X5dKkAAAAF29d0D5:20221116193026:s.

Hard work has become a negative concept, or a four-letter word, to some segments of the population. This kind of thinking leads many to become financially unstable. It's lazy and foolish thinking, but it's become so ingrained in our culture that many people probably don't even realize they're doing it. Too many assume that someone else will care for them or that the government will swoop in and save them. From what we discussed about Social Security and the national debt, it's obvious that won't happen. This mindset is almost like a disease, but it also presents an opportunity.

I see this trend and think that it's great for my kids. If I can instill in them the importance of work—being the first to arrive and the last to leave, putting in extra hours on nights and weekends—while others their age do the least amount possible, this gives them an advantage. Why? Because there will be less competition. They will stand out, get promoted faster, and make more money. The same can be true for you and your children.

Who would you promote if you were in charge: the Quiet Quitter or the employee working hard and making the most impact? Who would you give a raise to? You can use this trend to your advantage. Work hard now, be more secure, and live a more fulfilled life when it matters most. However, not everyone shares that sentiment, not even those I am closest to.

My family recently sat down to have lunch with friends we have known for thirty years. Our kids all grew up together and then went off to college, so it was nice to have everyone at the same table again. As we talked, one of our friends said they were upset because their son, who had just landed his first job out of college, had to work on a Saturday for a few hours. In front of the entire group, they told their son, "I'm so sorry. Maybe you should quit and find something else." Their opinion was that their kid shouldn't have to work so hard.

I kept my mouth shut. I didn't argue or say anything at all. I cringed the entire time, but I know my friends. They come from privilege and are huge consumers. They never had to work for a living, so they never developed that mentality. It made sense given their background and personal experience, but hearing that attitude spoken so brazenly was jarring. As soon as lunch ended, I took my kids aside and told them, "Don't listen to that nonsense."

The last thing I want is for my kids to get a negative idea about work. If anything, I want them to be prepared to work two jobs, and the reason for this goes far beyond making more money.

THE TRUE BENEFITS OF HARD WORK

Hard work is the best way to protect yourself from the Great Conflux and secure your future, but it's a declining trend among today's youth. According to CareerBuilder, the number of jobs held by teenagers between 2001 and 2014 decreased by 33 percent.[77] It's important to note that this stat is also impacted by the growing number of those fifty-five and older who remain in the workforce, but there is no doubt that there has been a sharp decline in teenagers who want and can appreciate work.

Making extra cash will help kids who have to save for college, but money isn't the only benefit for kids who get jobs. It's not even about the hard skills they learn at a job that is most beneficial; it's about how work prepares them for life. According to the US Department of Labor, every year a person works in their teens raises their income

---

[77] Dianna Miller, "Teen Employment Has Many Benefits," Youth First, July 4, 2017, https://youthfirstinc.org/teen-employment-many-benefits/.

by 14 to 16 percent in their twenties.[78] Work increases the likelihood a child will graduate from high school and reduces the risk of them becoming involved in criminal activity. The only catch is that the job can't interfere with their schoolwork because it can then become counterproductive.

When a teenager receives a paycheck for the first time, they can't help but develop a new appreciation for the value of money and learn how to budget. It teaches them a series of soft skills they will need throughout their lives, such as responsibility, creative thinking, problem-solving, time management, teamwork, organization, and communication. They get used to working for a boss and dealing with conflicts. They can build their network of contacts and references while expanding their circle of friends.

I can promise you that this is true because I experienced it firsthand. Growing up, I worked two (sometimes three) summer jobs while attending school. I worked seventy- to ninety-hour weeks for decades and still put in between fifty- and ninety-hour work weeks today. Because I worked so hard in the past, I could and may slow down soon. I'm doing something I love, but that attitude was hardwired into me at a young age. Not only did I learn the value of hard work, but I also learned skills I carried with me throughout my career that I still benefit from today.

When I sold bubble gum, I learned about trends and margins. I saw what was popular with my age group. I saw what everyone wanted, bought up all that stock, and got people to pay more. Trends are incredibly powerful, and I utilized those skills and that knowledge when selling baseball cards in college. When Score came out with a rare Bo Jackson card in 1990 with a picture of him wearing shoulder

---

78 Dianna Miller, "Teen Employment Has Many Benefits," Youth First, July 4, 2017, https://youthfirstinc.org/teen-employment-many-benefits/.

pads and holding a bat over his shoulders, everyone had to have that card. It went from $0.50 to $20 overnight. I knew I could make a huge margin on that card, so I paid the general manager at Smart & Final to tell me when he got his shipment of baseball cards in. I then bought them all up when they landed on the shelf. You never knew what cards would be in the packs, but the profit margins on those in-demand cards were so high that I knew I'd get enough of them to make a killing.

I may have gained fifteen pounds when working as a waiter at CPK because I ate way too much barbecue chicken pizza, but that experience taught me how a well-run organization was engineered. Their system was unusual for a restaurant at that time. Before stepping on the floor as a waiter, I had to train for three weeks. I then had to have a certain score on a test that required I know every single item on the menu. Considering some of those menu items had twenty ingredients, that was no small feat. I can still tell you today what's in a Thai Chicken Pizza. Is that knowledge essential to what I do today? Absolutely not, but I learned what was required to run a profitable business.

One of the most important lessons I learned at CPK is that business is cyclical. Not every period will be the same, and there will be downtime. The real estate business is the exact same way. It requires you to hedge and have a defensive business plan. I quickly realized that if you're in a cyclical business and don't have a cycle-proof business plan, you're in trouble. I'd later call that my definition of insanity. That knowledge has been a major part of my success, and I wouldn't have learned that so young had I not worked at CPK.

Working at a restaurant is a great first job. Not only will a teenager meet a variety of very colorful people, but unless you plan to travel completely off the grid, there will always be restaurants wherever you go. These jobs are great to have when going through college, and if you work your way up as a server, you can also make a lot of money. This can be an excellent option for young people to fall back on while they try to pursue their career out of college or act as a backup plan if they are in between jobs.

No matter what job you work at a young age, the most valuable skill you can develop is discipline. When it comes to being more productive, making more money, and then saving and properly investing that money, no skill is more instrumental to your future success. Discipline will come up every step of the way for the rest of this book, because it will give you an advantage in everything you do. If you struggle with discipline, it can be incredibly difficult to suddenly change course, so I loaded these pages with tips and tricks that can help you develop more discipline or instill this trait in your children.

> *"Life requires trade-offs. It demands that you figure out how to work hard and trust that it will be worth it. It expects you to delay gratification and know the reward is worth waiting for. It needs you to be disciplined and self-controlled now so that you can be free ... to fulfill your destiny later."*
>
> —RYAN HOLIDAY

SETTING YOURSELF UP FOR SUCCESS

Getting started is often difficult because people don't know where to begin. Everyone wants a quick fix or the secret formula, but I can tell you that there isn't one. What I can give you are these seven tips to ensure that you have the best chance to succeed, but success will still require discipline and hard work.

#1. Read as Much as Possible

Many of these ideas I'm promoting in this book, along with many great ideas that can help you protect your family, safeguard your future, and achieve your dreams, are not new. I didn't come up with the idea of working hard and getting a second job. I owe much of the success I experienced to reading what other people had to say.

When I was young, I learned the most from Warren Buffett, and even he didn't make up the ideas he wrote about from thin air. He's claimed that he got 90 percent of his new ideas from what he read. Buffett said he purchased his first stock at eleven, but not before he read every book in his hometown library on investing. He tells the story of how, when he was starting out, he paid the people who delivered the *Wall Street Journal* to deliver it at three a.m. instead of eight a.m. This way, he could wake up at three a.m. and get all the information before anybody else so that he could act on it immediately when the stock market opened. He became obsessed with investing and making money, so that's the material he devoured before setting up his first investment partnership in his twenties.

The lesson is simple: the more you read, the more you learn, and the more you can use that information to your advantage. It can also help you capitalize on trends sooner, making it more likely you will benefit before everyone else hops on the bandwagon. The only catch is that for reading and information gathering to be effective, you must want to do it. If it feels like a chore, you aren't going to do it. That all starts by creating a habit and learning to change your behavior. If you can make reading a part of your daily routine, eventually it will become second nature.

> **Exercise:**
> Pick one news source that you will commit to start reading today. Ideally, you want something in your wheelhouse or preferred area of interest. If this is a new habit that you already know will be difficult for you to commit to, start small. Commit to ten minutes a day. Everyone has ten minutes they can spare. If you read for ten minutes a day long enough, the time will soon fly by, and you can expand that window.

"I read and think. So, I do more reading and thinking, and make less impulse decisions than most people in business."

—WARREN BUFFETT

#2. Find a Mentor

I've never had a face-to-face conversation with Warren Buffett. We've never met, but I devoured everything he wrote. I critically analyzed his suggestions against those made by other experts and quickly learned that Buffett was right. Because of that, I consider him a mentor, and even though he never took me under his wing, I've learned more from him than just about anyone else.

All my mentors were like that. They weren't people I met in person, but those who were vocal with their opinions, philosophies, and knowledge, so I followed them. Who is that person for you? Is there someone you work with or someone whose writing and work you admire that you consider a mentor? What's great about mentors is that you can have as many as you want. With the wealth of information so readily available, you have more opportunities than ever to learn from experts. Take advantage of it!

Sometimes the most powerful lessons come not from advice but through cautionary tales that hammer home what not to do. As much as we desire to follow in the footsteps of our mentors, there are people whose behavior we should make sure not to emulate. I have a name for those people. They're called anti-mentors, and sometimes they can be just as important as mentors.

My father was one of my anti-mentors. He made a reasonable middle-class income but gambled and spent all of what he earned, so he had no savings. Due to that experience, nobody ever had to explain to me the importance of saving money and not spending it on what I didn't need because I saw the disastrous consequences of consumerism firsthand. Look around at your inner circle, the people you work with, and those you associate with regularly to see if you have any anti-mentors in your midst who you can also learn from.

#3. Learn How to Utilize Your Time

We are a culture plagued by distraction. The device we carry in our pockets designed to make our lives simple and convenient can have the opposite effect and suck away our valuable time through meaningless and mindless activities. Social media is the best example, as pointless scrolling has led to many lost hours.

If you're easily distracted or sucked into your phone, look for ways to eliminate that distraction. Turn off your notifications. Put your phone on silent. When you sit down to work, read, or do what you need to do, put your phone out of arm's reach or on the other side of the room, so you can't instinctively pick it up and pull yourself away from the task at hand. One of the tricks to becoming more productive is to rid your environment of distractions.

money & morons

> **Exercise:**
> It's easy to underestimate how much time you waste during a normal day until you closely examine it. For the next three days, keep track of what you do and how you spend your time. Set your alarm every two hours, and record what you did with that time. Be honest with yourself and note if an activity that should have taken you half an hour ended up taking an hour or more because you got distracted online. When you examine how you spend your time more closely, you will suddenly see all these pockets and opportunities you didn't realize were there. If you find that you've spent an average of two hours on social media, devote that time to being more productive. Depending on what you want to do, that might involve joining a business, enrolling in an online class, starting a side business, or maybe just reading.

#4. Follow Trends and Get into Growth Industries

When I was on the cusp of starting my real estate business thirty years ago, I was in the coffee shop reading when I came across a story in the *Wall Street Journal* about a huge demographic shift that was underway and would lead many in the upcoming generation to become renters. I did a little more digging and decided to shift a large portion of my business into apartments, a sector of real estate that would soon have high demand. I didn't make that decision on a whim. It came from readily available information that I used to make a business decision with low risk and high reward. And it paid off!

becoming more productive

What upcoming trends can you take advantage of? In chapter 1, we discussed how people are living longer. Think about how that will play out over time. It will strain Social Security and Medicare but also create opportunities. We can infer from that trend that the world will need more healthcare professionals. That means demand for more doctors and nurses. That field is going to expand rapidly. Even if you don't want to attend medical school, you can become a nurse practitioner or registered nurse. That requires less school, so it's a more affordable path to making more than $200,000 a year.

Some of you may be old enough to remember when Blockbuster Video ruled the video rental industry. That was when you had to drive to the video store to rent physical tapes and DVDs. Netflix started to change the game with a new business model that shipped DVDs directly to your home, so you didn't need to leave the house. It grew in popularity, and in 2000, Blockbuster had the chance to purchase Netflix for only $50 million. They declined, and that enormous miscalculation was the beginning of their demise. Netflix soon became their primary competitor and was better suited to transition to the next phase of the rental industry: streaming.

The world changes constantly, and industries change along with it. That change is inevitable and can ruin entire industries that are not prepared. Trends can foreshadow which industries will grow and which will slowly die. And if you are working in those dying sectors, it would be wise to plan your exit. Here is a brief and limited list of industries that are on the decline:

- Dirty energy
- Textiles
- Printed newspapers
- Heavy manufacturing in high-cost labor markets
- Mining in the United States

- Tobacco and related businesses
- Retail stores that are not convenience or service based

Trends can also foreshadow fluctuations within a single industry. Once again, reading allowed me to spot the red flag before the 2008 housing crisis. I wasn't in the business of selling single-family homes, but that sector can create a lot of contagion in the real estate world. I watched that trend carefully and took the advice of sector specialists to exit certain investments and put various hedges in place to avoid distress in our business. I wasn't lucky. I didn't have to guess. I knew it was coming because of the information I consumed. It sometimes really is that simple.

#5. Develop Multiple Sources of Income

There is no way around it—you must make more money to secure your future. Unfortunately, many people are limited by age, education, location, and work history. Here are some simple (and only a few of many) ways that anyone could use to make some extra money today:

- Take advantage of the gig economy: In your extra time, you can use your car to drive for Uber or Lyft or deliver food for DoorDash or Postmates.
- Take surveys: Depending on where you live, you can sign up for surveys and be part of focus groups. These services often pay per session.
- Sell or resell products online: Our houses are filled with clothes, devices, tools, and general items we don't need or no longer use. Instead of keeping them around to collect dust, consider selling them on a site such as OfferUp.
- Rent out your car or home: Consider renting your home on Airbnb or your car on Turo. Depending on your situation,

this is a simple way to make passive income with your assets when they aren't in use.
- Convert your garage or spare room into a rental unit: We'll discuss real estate in more detail later, but this is a great way to turn your home into a productive asset that lets you earn income through rent.
- Look for a problem people have and find a solution they are willing to pay for: Do you have a neighbor who will pay you to clean their gutters or their garage?

We can include product testing, research studies, mystery shopping—the list goes on and on and on. Because of the internet, especially with the advent of Web3, there are more ways to make money today than ever. It often requires developing the proper skills.

Technical or vocational training is an excellent way to learn a skilled trade and gain hands-on experience and practical training to become a mechanic or a plumber or to work in electronics, construction, food, service, manufacturing, or accounting. However, there are more ways than ever to supplement your income, and internet-based businesses have become huge moneymakers for many.

If you have writing or editing skills, freelancing is an excellent way to supplement your income or jump-start an entirely new career path. Affiliate marketing and e-commerce have become lucrative avenues and ways for many to make extra money in their spare time. What makes these options more viable than ever is that you can use the internet to further develop the necessary skills and learn how to use them to make more money. Online education is booming, and often all the information you need can be found for free on YouTube. All it takes is a little research, and you can quickly learn the lay of the land and determine an alternative path forward.

#6. Become an Expert

While low-paying and unskilled jobs can serve a function and are an excellent way for younger people to acquire the soft skills required to excel in the workforce, you don't want to be stuck doing that job forever. You always want to improve and develop skills that society needs and values. Once you figure out an area you want to pursue and a path forward, you must invest the time to become great at that pursuit.

In his 2008 book, *Outliers*, Malcolm Gladwell explains how one must invest ten thousand hours to become an expert at something. There has been criticism of this approach, and it's often misunderstood, but Gladwell has reiterated that this is not a hard-and-fast rule. It doesn't mean talent doesn't matter, and he has said there are certain areas where the rule doesn't translate as well, such as athletics, but I firmly believe in his basic premise. While the actual time may vary depending on the person and the skill they are trying to master, the rule is meant to be a metaphor for commitment and discipline when developing a skill set.

Mastery often takes longer than expected (typically ten years), but not all hours are created equal. You can't go through the motions. It's about practice, repetition, effort, and gaining experience. That's how one builds expertise. So, if you're in a position where you need to make more money or find a better job, get off social media, stop watching TV, stop playing video games (unless you plan to become a coder or developer), cut back on your non-productive socializing, and use that time to become an expert in an area that you know will grow.

#7. Invest in Yourself

This advice means nothing if you aren't healthy enough to enjoy it. The best thing you can do for your long-term security and that of your family is to take care of yourself mentally and physically. You must care for your body, eat well, exercise, and get enough sleep. You are and will always be your most valuable asset, so that comes first. And the healthier you are, the more equipped you will be to work hard and retain information. Investing in yourself will pay off more than any other investment because you will earn dividends for life.

* * *

If you kept track of how you typically spent your day, you probably discovered pockets of time that you could use to become more productive. How about you use some of that downtime to create a second source of income? You don't need to pick one of these ideas listed, and you don't need to devote all your free time to this pursuit. Get creative and see how you can take home a little more cash. Also, look for ways to kill two birds with one stone. If you commute, ride an exercise bike, or walk on the treadmill, you can listen to audiobooks or podcasts in your area of interest to gain a little more knowledge.

Many of these techniques can be implemented with planning and a well-organized schedule. Remember that you're playing the long game. If you want to enact change and develop wealth, it starts with the little things you do daily that add up over time. Set aside some time to read and educate yourself every day. Network and find a mentor. These are all ways to acquire information that will allow you to get ahead.

> **Being more productive and earning more money is not about making big, sweeping changes and waiting to land a high-paying job—it often comes down to the little things.**

Being more productive and earning more money is not about making big, sweeping changes and waiting to land a high-paying job—it often comes down to the little things. It's about doing just a few things in your daily life slightly differently and consistently over time. The first step is self-awareness. Too many people aren't aware of how their behavior and habits are holding them back and preventing them from creating the type of change they desire. Once you know how you might be wasting time or not living up to your potential, you can make those small, incremental changes. That can help you build momentum and eventually create the life you desire.

Once you become more productive and earn more money, you're ready to progress to the next step because you don't want to make the same mistake as many other Americans and not have anything to show for your hard work. You want to keep your money and put it to work so it can grow. You do that through saving.

KEY TAKEAWAYS

- By living in the United States, you have more opportunities than most. There is a reason why we only have 4 percent of the population and 40 percent of the millionaires. It's up to you whether you can take advantage of it.
- Securing your future begins with hard work. If you aren't willing to do the work, the rest doesn't matter. Trying to do as little as possible or only enough to get by will prevent you from succeeding.
- There is no such thing as a dead-end job. I have learned valuable lessons from every job I've held that I've brought with me and applied throughout my career.
- How to set yourself up for success:

1. Read as much as possible: The more you read, the more you learn, and the more you can use that information to your advantage.
2. Find a mentor: It doesn't need to be someone who you know or who takes you under their wing. Find someone whose work you admire and learn everything you can from that person.
3. Learn how to utilize your time: Time is your most precious resource. Keep track of how you spend your time and work to eliminate waste.
4. Follow trends and get into growth industries: Make sure you're setting yourself up for financial success by being able to spot trends and avoid dying industries.
5. Develop multiple sources of income: This can be in the form of a second job or supplemental income you earn in your spare time.
6. Become an expert: Invest the ten thousand hours required to master any skill.
7. Invest in yourself: Take care of yourself. Without your physical or mental health, you have nothing.

CHAPTER 5

saving: the art of financial discipline

"The more your money works for you, the less you have to work for money."

-IDOWU KOYENIKAN

"I only make $30,000 a year. How can I expect to save any money?"

That's a common concern. Most people assume that they can never save and invest because they don't make enough money. Whenever I hear people talk like that, I think of Ronald Reed. You have no reason to know his name, but Reed was a gas station attendant and janitor at JCPenney in Brattleboro, Vermont, who passed away in 2014 at the age of ninety-two. What's unusual is that he was worth $8 million when he died.[79] He didn't inherit his money—he was the first person in his family to graduate high school. He didn't make much,

---

79 Kathleen Elkins, "A Janitor Secretly Amassed an $8 Million Fortune and Left Most of It to His Library and Hospital," CNBC, August 29, 2016, https://www.cnbc.com/2016/08/29/janitor-secretly-amassed-an-8-million-fortune.html.

121

but he had two jobs, worked hard, saved what he made, and invested it wisely. He made his fortune quietly. When he died, even those closest to him didn't realize he was a multimillionaire.

Reed is living proof that the concepts and principles in this section work. He didn't spend money on things he didn't need. When he was thirty-eight years old, he bought a two-bedroom house for $12,000 and lived there his entire life. He drove a secondhand car and cut his own firewood. He was also a lifelong learner who read regularly, so he knew how to invest wisely. He took advantage of compounding, but not every strategy paid off. Of course, some of his investments lost money, but he always had plenty of money because he created sound habits. That's how he became so wealthy.

Whether you make $50,000 a year or $500,000, you can always argue that you aren't making enough money. It all comes down to learning how to live within your means. You don't need to wait to strike it rich or reach a certain income threshold to start saving.

This isn't rocket science. Learning what you need to do isn't difficult. Yes, saving and investing your money is easier if you start young, but that doesn't mean it's hopeless if you've already reached middle age. It's hard, but it can be done. However, it's impossible if you don't even start. Even though many of these principles we're going to discuss are simple, they do require financial and personal discipline, and unfortunately, that's an area where many Americans fall short. There is no better indication of that than the catastrophic savings rate in this country.

According to a November 2021 report,[80] 60 percent of Americans are living paycheck to paycheck, and 55 percent don't have $2,000

---

[80] "New Reality Check: The Paycheck-to-Paycheck Report," Lending Club, December 2022, https://www.pymnts.com/wp-content/uploads/2022/12/PYMNTS-New-Reality-Check-December-2022.pdf.

saved for a medical emergency. Savings rates may have increased when stimulus payments were distributed during the COVID-19 pandemic, but they quickly plummeted in the two years that followed while consumer and credit card loans skyrocketed.

Personal Savings Near Historical Bottom[81]

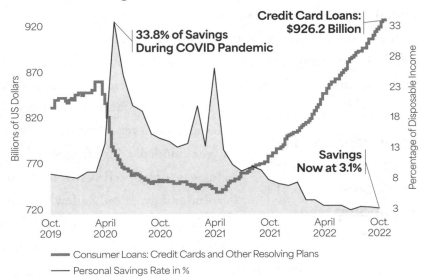

When the stimulus checks stopped going out, we quickly went from one of the highest savings rates in decades to the lowest. According to New York Life's Wealth Watch survey, more and more Americans dipped into their savings in 2022, taking out an average of $616.73. But it's not just savings accounts that are taking a hit. Many Americans have also dipped into their 401(k) and IRA accounts to help ease the burden.[82] People can blame it on the high cost of

---

81 Source: Bloomberg, Lombard Odier

82 Amber Hoffman, "Americans Gambling with Their Finances: Half of Americans Live Paycheck to Paycheck," NY Sports Day, November 29, 2022, https://www.nysports-day.com/2022/11/01/personal-finance-statistics/.

123

living, but I don't buy that for a second. While those living paycheck to paycheck are more impacted by inflation, they aren't the only ones unprepared for the future. Many who make over six figures find themselves in a similar boat.

One of my oldest and closest friends became very successful. We both started with nothing. He worked hard and began to make upward of $400,000 a year, so his wife stopped working about twenty years ago to focus on raising their children. We all remained distant friends, but one way that he became very different was that he spent his money freely. He loved the good life. That involved a big house, expensive cars, and many trips—Hawaii twice a year, skiing three times a year. Suddenly, his life took a turn. He was diagnosed with terminal cancer and given only a few years to live. If learning of a diagnosis like that wasn't bad enough, the family has little to no savings. They mistakenly assumed they were secure because they made such good money. They weren't. They didn't plan for the future and made the common mistake of assuming they had plenty of time to build their nest egg. Life will come with surprises. I guarantee it. You need to be prepared for them.

> **Americans' inability to save money is not an income issue; it's a spending issue.**

I feel for my friend. My heart goes out to him and his family. Money would not have impacted his diagnosis, but it would have given him peace of mind and helped prepare his family for life after he is gone. Unfortunately, my friend's financial situation is not unusual. It might be shocking to learn that almost 65 percent of people making over $100,000 have little to no savings and live paycheck to paycheck.[83] That makes it crystal clear that Americans' inability to save money is not an income issue; it's a spending issue. If you are making more than $100,000 a year and not saving and investing, that's moronic! It's important that I be blunt because the Great Conflux is coming. You can still prepare and protect yourself, your family, and your friends, but will you do that, or will you make excuses and wait for someone else to solve your problems?

This new phenomenon signifies that we're going down a dark path as a nation. If our high-income earners don't have savings and are living paycheck to paycheck, it means they can't be a part of the solution. That will put an even greater strain on themselves and the system.

CONSUMERISM IS A DISEASE

The best way to start saving more money is to spend less. Not spending $100 on something you don't need is the same as making $100. This should be a no-brainer, but society has conditioned us to become rabid consumers.

This isn't entirely your fault. Every day, we are bombarded with ads and messages to buy. Gap, Gucci, Costco, Lululemon, Zara—the list goes on and on and on. Companies spend billions of dollars to get you to buy what you don't need. They get rich off the money you should be saving for your future. That's where the money from all those stimulus checks went. Retail therapy has become an addiction.

---

83   Alexandre Tanzi, "Even on $100,000-Plus, More Americans Are Living Paycheck to Paycheck," Bloomberg, January 30, 2023, https://www.bloomberg.com/news/articles/2023-01-30/even-on-100k-plus-more-americans-live-paycheck-to-paycheck.

money & morons

The average person sees six thousand to ten thousand ads a day.[84] That's 219,000 to 365,000 ads a year. They are programming you to consume. Snap out of it!

Another reason I admire Warren Buffett is because he is the complete opposite of the typical American addicted to consumerism. I've followed him for thirty years, and the man still lives in the same house. He never bought a lavish mansion, and even though he could afford to live anywhere he wanted, he chose to live in a modest house.

If you think you're exempt from the disease of consumerism, take a minute to look around your home. Take note of every item you have that you don't need. Add to that all the shit you bought and threw away. Now imagine if you could trade those items in to get back the money you spent. Think of how much more you'd have in your account to start saving. Life doesn't work like that, but before you can be expected to correct the issue, you need to be aware of it. The retail industry spends billions of dollars a year in advertising that programs and conditions you to believe that brands are a status symbol and products will bring you happiness. That's bullshit, but you can't expect to treat the disease of consumerism if you don't even realize you're afflicted. The problem is that most people don't think they have a problem. You may or may not be one of those people, but there is only one way to find out. Let's get specific and help you understand exactly where your money goes.

Pull up your credit card and bank statements. Look at every dollar you've spent over the past twelve months. Add it all up and take stock of where your money is going. I want you to take a high-

---

84 Emilia Kirk, "The Attention Economy: Standing Out among the Noise," *Forbes*, March 23, 2022, https://www.forbes.com/sites/forbesbusinessdevelopmentcouncil/2022/03/23/the-attention-economy-standing-out-among-the-noise/?sh=c1efd897fda2.

saving: the art of financial discipline

lighter and outline every purchase you made that you didn't need and could be eliminated. What subscriptions might be on auto-renew that you didn't even realize were there? Is there a gym membership or a streaming service you're being charged for that you don't use? Are there any hidden bank fees on your statements that you haven't noticed? Those can occur if you take money from a nonaffiliated ATM or don't keep a certain balance in your account. How can you streamline your life and cut back on your spending?

If you really want this point to hit home, pull up your credit card statement from three years ago and see how many of those purchases are still relevant. Do you remember all the dinners you spent money on? Do you remember all those Amazon purchases? How many of the things you bought made a real impact on your life? How many will help you in retirement and save you from the Great Conflux?

Once you start thinking like this, you can train your brain to consider each purchase before you make it. This doesn't mean you can't buy things you want, but remember that not spending $100 is the same as making $100. The money you didn't spend and the money you earn both end up in the same account, and it doesn't matter how it got there.

Looking back over what you spent is how you become aware of the problem, but looking ahead to the future is how you correct the issue and become more economical with your spending. Get in the habit of tracking every single thing you purchase. Try it out for a week. Document it all. That includes the $100 phone bill and the $4 coffee you bought on the way to work. At the end of the week, look over everything you purchased. What can you easily cut out? What can you stop buying? If you spend too much on restaurants or takeout, see if you can start cooking more at home. If you spend way more money at Starbucks than you realized, invest in a coffee machine and start making your own.

What's great about this exercise is that it doesn't require significant life changes. You're simply eliminating the waste and cutting out the things you don't need. Most people succumb to consumerism because they don't realize where their money goes and how easily they can change their behavior. Self-awareness is half the battle and takes over much of the heavy lifting from discipline.

You can take this even further by getting close friends and family to help you. Think of how often you get gifts that you don't need for your birthday or holidays. One idea is to ask your close family and friends—those you know will give you something for a specific occasion—to give you a check instead. Don't spend that money—save it with the intention of investing. The chances are slim that a random gift will significantly change or improve your life, but the money you invest will grow over time. It may seem unsentimental, but it's a practical way to get your family and friends to help you create these habits required to get you on the right track.

SETTING YOURSELF UP FOR SUCCESS

If you are stuck and unsure where to begin, here are some simple tips and techniques to help you course correct, so you can save more of your money. I need to warn you again that this all requires discipline and hard work.

#1. Understanding Credit Cards

One of the worst tools of consumerism is credit cards. They can be valuable if you make your payments on time, don't carry an outstanding balance, and utilize points. But if you don't and wind up paying interest on your outstanding balance, you're throwing your money away. Unfortunately, as inflation drives up the price of everyday

saving: the art of financial discipline

goods, many Americans rely on credit cards to lessen the burden. According to the Federal Reserve Bank of New York, credit card balances escalated by $38 billion during the third quarter of 2022.

Living paycheck to paycheck makes it significantly easier to fall into credit card debt. Those in debt aren't oblivious, as 24 percent of those in financial trouble cite paying off their debt as their most important financial goal,[85] but once you fall into that trap, you're setting yourself up for failure because the interest rates are so incredibly high.

Usury laws regulate the amount of interest that can be charged for a loan, but credit is a different beast entirely, and credit card companies aren't subject to the same regulation. The reason is that, unlike a mortgage or car loan, the bank has little power or collateral to collect from someone who doesn't pay their credit card balance. And unlike a house or a car, the bank can't take back the food you bought at the grocery store or the trip you went on the previous month. That makes it much more of a risk for a lender, which is why credit cards can charge up to 22 percent interest on your outstanding balance. No other lender can legally charge that much.

Usury laws differ per state, and credit card companies take advantage of that by incorporating in states such as Delaware and South Dakota because they have the laxest usury laws. And the law applies to the company's home state, not yours.

The annual percentage rate (APR) that credit card companies can charge you will depend on your credit. Those with the best credit

---

85 "More Than Half of Paycheck-to-Paycheck Consumers Say Inflation's Made It Harder to Meet Long-Term Financial Goals," PYMNTS, December 15, 2022, https://www.pymnts.com/consumer-finance/2022/more-than-half-of-paycheck-to-paycheck-consumers-say-inflations-made-it-harder-to-meet-long-term-financial-goals/#:~:text=Financially%20struggling%20consumers%20are%20the%20most%20likely%20to%20cite%20paying,not%20living%20paycheck%20to%20paycheck.

might get a rate closer to 10 percent, while those with poor credit could be charged as much as 22 percent. That is the amount charged to any outstanding balance. Only a few percentage points can translate to you paying thousands more dollars over time, but I'd argue that even 10 percent is too high to be paying. You don't want to *ever* pay any interest, which is why you *never* want to pay the minimum balance on your credit card bills. You are literally throwing your money away, and all those things you're purchasing that you don't need to end up costing you two or three times the sticker price. That can increase your money troubles exponentially and get you into a hole that is difficult to dig yourself out of.

> **Debt comes in many forms, including home mortgages, car loans, and student loans, but the most dangerous and destructive form of debt is credit card debt.**

If you can't pay off your credit card balance every month, you're spending too much money. It's a clear sign that you are living beyond your means, and if you have cut back on your spending and still struggle to pay for the cost of living, you need to find ways to become more productive and make more money. However, if you're already in debt, this becomes a much more difficult task, but it's certainly not impossible.

#2. Getting Out of Debt

When saving your money and safeguarding your future, one big elephant in the room must be addressed: debt.

saving: the art of financial discipline

At the end of 2022, consumer debt rose $1.3 trillion from the previous year to a record $16.9 trillion.[86] Debt comes in many forms, including home mortgages, car loans, and student loans, but the most dangerous and destructive form of debt is credit card debt because it's the result of people buying products they don't need, and the interest rates are so ridiculously high.

According to the Urban Institute, as of August 2021, more than 64 million Americans with a credit report (28 percent of the country) had debt in collections on their report.[87] If a college education and purchasing a home puts most people in debt, consumerism adds gasoline to a fire that burns so hot, many Americans fear they will never be able to put it out. If you want to secure your future, you *need* to get out of debt, but how?

Step number one is to curb your spending. If you hold multiple debts, step two is to pay off the debt with the highest interest rate. That's it—just pay off one debt at a time. If you have money left over, or when that debt is paid off, start paying off the debt with the next-highest interest rate. This technique, called the debt avalanche, helps you pay off your debt the fastest. It's tempting to pay off the smallest debt by dollar amount first (referred to as the debt snowball) because this approach gives you small psychological wins that create the illusion of progress, but it will take you longer to pay off, and you will pay more money in interest. It all goes back to discipline. Everything in this section traces back to discipline.

---

86 Jeff Cox, "Consumer Debt Hits Record $16.9 Trillion as Delinquencies Also Rise," CNBC, February 16, 2023, https://www.cnbc.com/2023/02/16/consumer-debt-hits-record-16point9-trillion-as-delinquencies-rise-as-well.html.

87 Alexander Carther, Caleb Quakenbush, and Signe-Mary McKernan, "The Number of Americans with Debt in Collections Fell during the Pandemic to 64 Million," Urban Wire, March 21, 2022, https://www.urban.org/urban-wire/number-americans-debt-collections-fell-during-pandemic-64-million.

Once you've managed to pull yourself out of debt, you can get to work repairing your credit. You need good credit to secure a business loan, lower your interest rate, and build your future. The best thing you can do is always pay off your credit card balances in full and never miss payments. If you want to speed up that process and raise your credit score, you can implement two simple approaches immediately.

1. Become an authorized user: If you have a friend or family member with good credit, you can become an authorized user on their account. This person needs to trust you because it means you can access their account, but you don't even need to have the card or know the account number. Just being an authorized user allows you to piggyback on their good credit. What's great about this approach is that your poor credit can't impact their good credit, so they don't have any liability when helping you out. If you're a parent with good credit, get your children credit cards when they are young and teach them to pay off their balances every month and on time.
2. Raise your credit limits: If you pay your bills in full and on time, you can periodically raise your credit limits. You will increase your credit score if you have a high credit allowance and low utilization. And higher limits also increase your borrowing power.

#3. Savings Strategies

If you struggle to save and don't know where to begin, you can use one of the most common percentage-based budget strategies: the 50/30/20 Rule. It's simple. Break down your income into three categories. Dedicate 50 percent to needs, 30 percent to wants, and 20 percent to savings/investing.

saving: the art of financial discipline

Needs include bills and what it costs to live and survive. Wants are things you don't need, such as a night out at a restaurant, or better versions of what you need, such as a fancier car. Savings and investing fit into that final category. You put that money away and don't touch it. Some people consider debt payment part of saving and investing, but given how much of a burden debt becomes, I would place that in the first category of needs. You'll thank me because the sooner you pay off the debt, the less you'll pay in interest and the more money you will have in your account.

This sounds simple on paper, but certain variables—especially how much money you make and where you live—can make this more difficult. It may cost some people more than 50 percent of their income to live. If that's the case, you simply adjust the percentages. And if you're already deep in debt, or struggling to pay your bills every month, you need to shrink that 30 percent dedicated to wants until you can make more money. It sounds harsh and will require some sacrifice in the short term, but it's not nearly as harsh as living the rest of your life poor and in debt, so you have a choice.

Ultimately, the exact percentage doesn't matter; the practice itself and the discipline required to stick to it are what's most important. Just make sure you're being honest with yourself about what you absolutely "need." That's true discipline, and if you need some help getting started, you can begin automating your savings. If you get a regular paycheck, get in the habit of having a certain percentage of your money automatically deposited into a savings account. Once you get into the habit of compartmentalizing the money you have coming in, you make this process easier on yourself because it's automatic. You no longer have to think about it.

As you save more money, you can consider additional savings vehicles. Traditional bank interest is around 0.03 percent, which might not come close to keeping up with the price of inflation. If you keep a significant amount of your money in a savings account, it will decrease in value over time. The convenience of a savings account is that you can access your money and take out as much as you want without incurring any of the penalties or fees you will pay if you withdraw money from many of the investment vehicles we will discuss in the next chapter. You have many options for where to put your money, but one of the simplest is a high-yield savings account. Interest rates change quickly, but these accounts range from 2.5 to 4.5 percent. That's not as high as the investment options we will discuss, but it's much better than traditional bank interest. It's also a good option for an emergency fund that you want to access quickly and withdraw money from without any financial penalty.

The earlier you start saving, the more money you'll accumulate and the better off you'll be because you'll have more options. The most profitable and productive option you can take advantage of is step three: investing that money. If you don't invest your money and keep it in cash or in a traditional bank account, inflation will cause your money to lose its purchasing power, so it will be worth a little less two, three, or ten-plus years down the line. What you want is to use your money to make more money. Properly investing your money to purchase assets will help you combat inflation while also making a significant profit. That's the beauty of investing.

KEY TAKEAWAYS

- Saving is a mindset. You don't need to make a lot of money to begin saving. You just need to learn to live within your means. Savings isn't a problem only for those who don't make much

money. Of the people making over $100,000, 65 percent have little to no savings and live paycheck to paycheck.
- Consumerism is a disease. Not spending $100 is the same as earning $100. Don't waste your money on things you don't need.
- Keep track of everything you spend. It's easy to underestimate how much money you waste, but when you see every purchase laid out in front of you, it becomes much easier to come up with a plan for how to increase your savings.
- How to set yourself up for success:
    1. Understanding credit cards: Don't let bad credit drag you down. Pay your bill in full every month. Otherwise, you are throwing your money away by paying interest. And if you can't pay your bill in full every month, it's a sign that you are spending too much.
    2. Get out of debt: Before you can expect to save money, you need to pull yourself out of debt. That needs to become priority number one because bad debt will prevent you from putting your money to work for you and building wealth.
    3. Come up with a savings strategy and put away a certain percentage of the money you make every month: By making saving automatic, you no longer have to think about it.

CHAPTER 6

investing: how to secure your future

"Risk comes from not knowing what you are doing."

—WARREN BUFFETT

I started investing in the stock market at seventeen, and it was not pretty. My timing was terrible, and I had zero market knowledge. What I was doing was more speculation than investing. You can't speculate when you invest. If you do, it's just gambling. You must educate yourself if you invest a significant portion of your money because there are no sure things. Consider a company like Apple. It's easy to think that you can make a lot of money investing in Apple stock, which you can, but it's not guaranteed. I have lost money on that stock thirteen times. Since I began investing, I have experienced long periods where I lost more money in the stock market than I made, which is why educating yourself is priority number one. If you don't know what you're doing, you're setting yourself up for failure. Luckily, there are more opportunities today to educate yourself than ever before.

Founded in 2013, Robinhood is an online trading app that makes buying and selling stocks simple and easy for everyone. They even skip some of the steps other firms require and have expanded their services beyond trading stocks by adding options trading and margin loans. It was a good idea, and it took off! In the first three months of 2020, Robinhood users traded nine times as many shares as E-Trade customers and forty times as many as Charles Schwab customers.[88]

What's the problem? More people with access to the market is good, right? Well, not if those people have no idea what they're doing. It's easy for inexperienced investors to find themselves in over their heads, and while they can quickly make money, they can lose it all just as fast. And those losses can be devastating.

In 2017, Navy medic Richard Dobaste signed up for Robinhood and funded his account with $15,000 in credit card advances before he started quickly trading risky stocks. He lost money and took out $60,000 in home equity loans to keep trading. It worked for a while, and his account grew to over $1 million, but he then lost $860,000 in a single month before his account dropped below $7,000. These drastic swings are more than many people can afford and psychologically handle. Twenty-year-old Nebraska college student Alex Kearns took his own life when he saw his Robinhood account drop to negative $730,000.

These are extreme cases, but it shows how much trouble uninformed traders can get into. If you're investing in risky stocks without doing your homework, you might as well be gambling. Rule number one is not to treat investing like a game of chance and to understand the playing field before you join the game.

---

[88] Nathaniel Popper, "Robinhood Has Lured Young Traders, Sometimes with Devastating Results," *New York Times*, September 25, 2021, https://www.nytimes.com/2020/07/08/technology/robinhood-risky-trading.html.

THE FUNDAMENTAL PRINCIPLES OF INVESTING

Much like making and saving money, discipline and reading to educate yourself are prerequisites. After that, there are five tenets that every good investor must learn to utilize:

1. Compounding
2. Diversification
3. Consistency
4. Using the government
5. Patience

#1. Compounding

The first and most important lesson to learn about investing is the power of compounding. Once this sinks in, it's life-changing. Albert Einstein said, "Compound interest is the eighth wonder of the world. He who understands it, earns it; he who doesn't, pays it!" Einstein was no financial guru, but he could recognize the power of this tool. Compounding is powerful and must be understood, yet few novice investors do.

Here's a test. Would you rather have a million dollars or receive a penny doubled every day for thirty-one days? It's easy to say that you'd take the million dollars, but when you do the math, a penny doubled every day for thirty-one days comes to $10,737,418.24. It's not even close, and the reason is because of the power of compounding.

Put simply, compounding is when your interest earns interest. It's a snowball effect that helps you earn more money over time. The best way to understand compounding is to see it for yourself.

money & morons

Let's say you have $10,000 that you keep in a safe in your house, and every month you add $500 to that safe. In twenty years, you'll have $130,000 saved up. That's not bad, but because of inflation, in twenty years, $130,000 will not be worth what it is today. More significantly, you're missing out on building true wealth because you aren't compounding. Let's take those same figures and see the difference if you keep that same amount in an account for twenty years and earn only 1 percent interest.

Initial Investment:	$10,000
Monthly Contribution:	$500
Length of Time in Years:	20
Estimated Interest Rate:	1%
Compound Frequency:	Annually
Investment after Twenty Years:	$144,315.92

That's a little bit more money than the $130,000 you'd have when not compounding, but let's run those same numbers and assume you make the average market return of 8 percent.

Initial Investment:	$10,000
Monthly Contribution:	$500
Length of Time in Years:	20
Estimated Interest Rate:	8%
Compound Frequency:	Annually
Investment after Twenty Years:	$321,181.36

That's good, and almost three times what you would make by keeping your money at home in a safe, but what if you can consistently beat the market and earn 15 percent interest? How much would you have after twenty years?

Initial Investment:	$10,000
Monthly Contribution:	$500
Length of Time in Years:	20
Estimated Interest Rate:	15%
Compound Frequency:	Annually
Investment after Twenty Years:	$945,744.68

Compare that to the $130,000 you'd have when not compounding and you can see how this is really a superpower, but don't only take my word for it. You can run the numbers yourself and plug in any figures and percentages you want to see what you could earn. Two compound interest calculators can be found at:

https://www.investor.gov/financial-tools-calculators/calculators/compound-interest-calculator

https://www.nerdwallet.com/banking/calculator/compound-interest-calculator

A simple way to wrap your head around compounding is the Rule of 72. It works like this: divide seventy-two by your average rate of return. So, if you take seventy-two and divide it by the average rate of return for the stock market (8 percent), you get nine. That's how many years it will take for you to double your money. Now, let's say that your rate is fourteen percent. Divide seventy-two by that, and it will only take five years.

That's a little trick that can help you figure out how compounding works and better understand how increasing your rate of return by only a few percentage points can significantly impact your wealth. If your money doubles every five years instead of every nine years over an extended period, that can result in millions of dollars.

Many people will tell you that it's hard to grow your money a percentage higher than the average annual rate of return, and it is, but it can be done. I have grown my investments at about 25 percent a year for the last thirty years. Warren Buffet's rate of return is much higher. The fundamentals discussed in this book will help you get started on that path.

#2. Diversification

I learned working at CPK that business is cyclical. Learning that at a young age benefited me when I transitioned into real estate. It also helped me when I began investing. It doesn't matter if you're investing in stocks, bonds, real estate, or cattle; you will experience a severe downturn at some point. The only way you can hedge against those downturns is through diversification. That involves spreading out your investments so you don't have too much riding on a single investment or in a single industry or sector.

The basic rule of thumb is to never put more than 10 percent of your capital into a single investment, whether a stock, a bond, real estate, or a piece of art.

#3. Consistency

Work hard, save, invest; repeat.

If you can consistently do this over time, you will secure your future and protect yourself from the Great Conflux. It's really that simple. What's difficult is the discipline required to do it regularly, not dip into the profits, and not spend your money on things you don't need. That allows you to reinvest your dividends or profits, and only then can you take advantage of the modern miracle that is compounding.

#4. Using the Government

Just because the government makes moronic decisions doesn't mean you must follow suit. Those moronic decisions might hurt us all down the line, but when the government printing press is alive and well, you can use it to your advantage. If you know how, the government can help you in meaningful ways. Here are a few examples.

Investing

If you receive a stimulus check, don't blow that money on things you don't need. Save it and invest it. With the power of compounding, that government handout can double. Inflation may destroy the middle class, but it's great for investing, especially in hard assets that produce income. If you aren't investing, you're only suffering from inflation and not benefiting.

This concept goes back to diversification. When you see inflation on the horizon, you need to hedge. In my business, that means investing in commodities such as lumber and steel. Those commodities tripled in pricing in the wake of inflation. If you can spot the trends, you can do very well because it's during downturns that there is the greatest opportunity.

Small Business Association (SBA)

If you live in a city, you've probably seen those carts on the roadside that sell fruit. It can vary, but those carts typically make $25,000 a year after the cost of fruit and labor. If you subtract the cost of the cart, you're still looking at a profit of over $20,000 per year for one cart. Now, imagine if you buy twenty carts. That's a nice little business that nets you about $400,000 a year while only costing you $100,000.

I can already hear the question: "I don't have that kind of money to buy twenty fruit carts." Most people don't, but you don't have to because you can get a loan from the SBA. You need good credit, but you don't need a lot of savings or a high income. You only need to prove you're responsible and not already in debt.

If you feel stuck making minimum wage and want to break the cycle, the SBA is an excellent way to do it because they benefit from all this money printing. You can keep your regular job and use this as an ancillary form of income. Of course, there are licensing and regulations you need to consider before pursuing the example above, and you may not live in an area where this would be profitable, but it's a simple illustration of how you can utilize the government to start your own business. You're not only helping yourself—50 percent of all new jobs in the United States are created by small businesses, not big corporations. The only catch is that you have to work really hard.

> **There is no shortcut or easy way to secure your future or reliably build wealth without taking big risks.**

#5. Discipline and Patience

"No matter how great the talent or effort, some things just take time. You can't produce a baby in one month by getting nine women pregnant."

That's another Warren Buffett quote that says something incredibly profound in only a single sentence. You can't expect anything we've discussed to happen overnight. There is no shortcut or easy way to secure your future or reliably build wealth without taking big risks. It all takes time, and your behavior will determine your success. If you haven't lived with this type of financial discipline and patience, it might be difficult initially, but you must change your habits. When you change your habits, you change your behavior, and pretty soon, the discipline that was once so difficult will come naturally. You'll work hard, save, and invest without thinking about it. Now all you need to know is where to put that money so it will grow.

BASIC INVESTMENT VEHICLES

The options may seem overwhelming when starting out, so you want to keep it simple. When I talk of investing, I'm not suggesting that you start day-trading stocks on your own. You don't want to do that—very few people should do that. The risk is far too high, and if you don't know what you're doing, it's much too easy to lose your money. When investing, you want to minimize risk and maximize reward consistently over an extended period. These are the vehicles that best allow you to do that.

401(k)

The government has created this tax-advantaged account as a way for employers to help employees save for retirement.

Each employee sets an amount or a percentage to be deducted from their taxable income and deposited into their 401(k) account. That money is not taxed, so if you make $100,000 a year and contribute $5,000, your taxable income is $95,000. Not only does contributing to a 401(k) account decrease the percentage of your income that you pay in taxes, but that money also grows tax-deferred while in that account. You don't pay any taxes until you take it out during retirement, so your money can compound without being taxed. The only catch is that you can't take it out before age 59.5 without suffering penalties and fees.

What makes 401(k) accounts such a good investment vehicle is that some employers agree to match their employees' contributions. That means if you contribute $5,000 a year, they will match that $5,000, and you will have $10,000 in your retirement account at the end of the year. Policies differ among employers, and there may be limits, but that's free money. It's in your best interest to contribute as much as possible. If you've worked for different companies, you might have multiple 401(k)s, but you can combine them through a rollover into your current 401(k) or IRA without suffering any penalties.

It sounds crazy, but many employees don't take full advantage of their 401(k) account or contribute at all. If your company offers this, contribute as much as you can afford, and plan to increase that contribution every year.

Individual Retirement Account (IRA)

If you're an independent contractor without an employer offering a 401(k), there are similar investing options so your money (and profits) won't be taxed when in a retirement account. When it comes to individual retirement accounts, or IRAs, there are two main types.

1. Traditional IRA: With a traditional IRA, your contribution is not taxed. This will reduce your annual taxable income, so you get a tax deduction up front. However, the money earned in the account will be taxed at the income rate when you withdraw it in retirement.
2. Roth IRA: With a Roth, the money you contribute has already been taxed, but the earnings are tax-free. That means when you withdraw the money during retirement, you don't need to pay any taxes on it.

Deciding between the two comes down to one simple question: Will your tax rate be higher now or in retirement? If you think it will be lower in retirement, go with the traditional IRA, but if you think it will be higher, go with the Roth.

investing: how to secure your future

If you want to diversify your tax savings, you can open a traditional IRA and a Roth. No matter which option you choose, you want to contribute early and often to maximize the benefits. Most importantly, you can't take the money out because if you withdraw before age 59.5, you will be subject to taxes and penalties, except in certain rare circumstances.

IRAs, 401(k)s, and Roth IRAs are powerful yet simple investment vehicles that will generate consistent returns over time. They also help young investors learn discipline. Regardless of the approach, you want to think of investing as a long game. As the graph below indicates, the longer you invest, the lower the risk.

The Longer You Invest, the Lower the Risk of Losing Money[89]

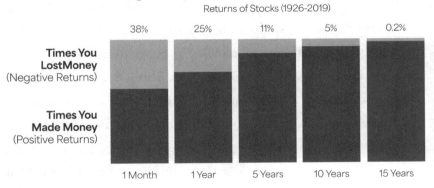

The other benefit of these vehicles, which makes them great investments to make early, is that they allow you to compound tax-deferred money. In other words, you don't pay taxes on this money until you take it out. The government has given us this incredible gift of tax-deferred savings, and people need to learn how to use this to their advantage.

---

89   Sarwa.co

Index Funds

If a stock is an ownership share in a single company, an index fund is a group of stocks that tracks a market index, such as the S&P 500. That's an index fund comprised of shares in all five hundred of these companies. Other examples of indexes that are tracked by an index fund include the Dow Jones Industrial Average (DJIA), the NASDAQ 1000, and the Russell 2000. There are several other funds comprised of various commodities, assets, and currencies.

Index funds are a passive investing strategy, meaning you don't have to worry about buying and selling the individual stocks within the fund when there are dips in the market. They also have higher long-term growth potential than most other investments, as there is a good chance that the funds will increase in value along with the market average. However, these funds aren't completely risk-free. As the market fluctuates, so does the index fund, and since the market increases at an average annual rate of 8 percent, the odds are in your favor that the fund will increase over time. This is a simple set-it-and-forget-it strategy to help you outpace inflation and earn a little more. On average, you can double your return in less than ten years.

Index funds are different from actively managed mutual funds, which are a collection of stocks specifically chosen by an investment manager. Mutual funds require the managers to make frequent (often hourly) decisions on which stocks they want to include in the fund. The idea is to constantly pick new investments that will generate the best returns, but human oversight is flawed, especially when dealing with a complex system such as the stock market. While the potential gains are higher in mutual funds, so are the potential losses.

Simply put, mutual funds are moronic. The results speak for themselves: 88.4 percent of mutual funds have underperformed their respective benchmark for the past fifteen years,[90] yet 49 percent of Americans have money in mutual funds. The average expense ratio charged by US mutual funds (the management fee paid by customers) is 0.71 percent. That alone doesn't sound like a big number, but 0.71 percent of the $23.9 trillion invested in mutual funds comes to $169.69 billion. That's what mutual funds make each year for managing your money and 88.4% of them are underperforming the market.[91]

Investors pay money managers a fee in the hope that mutual funds will outperform index funds, only for many of them to fall significantly short. Even if the fund does outperform the market, those fees cut into the investors' returns. That's why many experts consider mutual funds to be a racket.

If you want to invest intelligently, invest in index funds with low fees. That's not just my advice. Warren Buffet said, "When trillions of dollars are managed by Wall Streeters charging high fees, it will usually be the managers who reap outsized profits, not the clients. Both large and small investors should stick with low-cost index funds."

Before investing with a so-called expert in stocks, real estate, hedge funds, private equity, bonds, or venture capital, you want to ensure that the expert has a consistent track record of beating the market. Not for one, two, or even five years (because anyone can get lucky), but for decades. I know that's an extremely high bar, and few managers can generate those results, but they do exist. These managers

---

[90] Andrew Lanoie, "The Middle-Class Mindset of the High-Income Earners and the Block to Invest in Real Estate," *Forbes*, September 14, 2021, https://www.forbes.com/sites/forbesrealestatecouncil/2021/09/14/the-middle-class-mindset-of-the-high-income-earners-and-the-block-to-invest-in-real-estate/?sh=d37c408592e2.

[91] Andrew Lanoie, "The Middle-Class Mindset of the High-Income Earners and the Block to Invest in Real Estate," *Forbes*, September 14, 2021, https://www.forbes.com/sites/forbesrealestatecouncil/2021/09/14/the-middle-class-mindset-of-the-high-income-earners-and-the-block-to-invest-in-real-estate/?sh=d37c408592e2.

are worth their fees because, in the long run, they will make you more money and give you a higher rate of return.

Over the past fifteen years, only 10.62 percent of funds outperformed the S&P 500.[92] They are typically sector specialists who thoroughly understand the market. They also tend to have some of the business's strongest and most disciplined management teams. That's what allows them to execute at such a high level. Without one of those proven experts, the fees most money managers charge will dilute your returns and are not worth it. It can be difficult for the average person to access these funds, which is why reading and educating yourself is so important. It helps you better identify these opportunities and will take much of the guesswork out of your decision-making.

When choosing an index fund, you first want to open a brokerage account with a company like Vanguard, Fidelity, or Charles Schwab. Most brokers are commission free, and the sign-up process can easily be completed online. When choosing the right broker, consider the minimum investment, which can range from $0 to $3,000 or more, depending on the broker. Finally, compare the expense ratio (avoid paying more than 0.05 percent) and transaction fees, because this can also vary between brokers, but if you pick a fund, such as Schwab's S&P 500 Index Fund (SWPPX), it's in your best interest to go through Schwab's brokerage to avoid any fees. However, since the Schwab S&P 500 comprises the same stocks as Vanguard or Fidelity's S&P fund, there should be little to no difference in their performance.

---

[92] S&P Dow Jones Indices, "SPIVA Data Results by Region," S&P Global, https://www.spglobal.com/spdji/en/research-insights/spiva/.

> **Exercise:**
> Remember when you sifted through all your expenses to find waste and excess spending? Take half of that money (or take all of it) and open an investment account. That's it. That's all you have to do right now. Just get yourself in the game.

THE POWER OF PRODUCTIVE ASSETS

Everyone says that it's part of the American Dream to one day own your own home, but the reality is that a home is not a productive asset. That means it doesn't give you the highest possible value over time. Let me explain.

Yes, the value of a home will appreciate over time, and you gain equity, so you can turn around and sell it for more than you bought it, but guess what appreciates even more? An apartment building. Try thinking of it like this: Let's say you purchase a home and an apartment building, each for $100,000. Both will appreciate over time. However, the apartment building has the added benefit of providing income through rent, thus creating a second income stream. That's one of the reasons real estate is one of the most productive assets you can own and the best way to build true wealth, but it requires knowing the system.

You can make a lot of money buying and selling property, but large capital gains come with hefty taxes. The way to get around that is through 1031 exchanges, because they allow you to defer those taxes. The way it works is that instead of taking the profit from the sale of your property, you put it in a 1031 exchange so you don't have to pay taxes and can use that money to purchase a new home. You then have

money & morons

forty-five days to identify a new property of equal or greater value and 180 total days to complete the transaction on that property.

It's not tax-free money, but it is tax-deferred. You eventually have to pay taxes on the money you earned when you take the money out, but in the meantime, you can build wealth faster by using the money you would have paid in capital gain tax as funds to invest in a new property that is worth more and will give you a bigger return. A 1031 exchange is one of the best ways to keep all your money working for you, and you can do this repeatedly. There is no limit. Once you add the tax benefits of depreciation and 1031 exchanges, it makes a real estate investment, such as an apartment building, an extremely productive asset. See the graph below for an illustration of how your money grows in a home compared to an income-producing real estate investment.

	House	Rental Property
Purchase Price	$500,000	$500,000
Loan	$300,000	$300,000
Equity	$200,000	$200,000
Annual Income		$50,000
Taxes, Insurance, Utilities, Misc.	$9,000	$15,000
Loan Payments @ 7%[93]	$24,176	$24,176
Annual Cash Flow	($33,176)	$10,824
Property Value in Year 10[94]	$671,958	$671,958
Loan Payoff	$256,120	$256,120
Sale Proceeds	$415,838	$415,838
Initial Equity	$200,000	$200,000
Total Profit from Sale	$215,838	$215,838
Annual Cash Flow Over 10 Years	($331,759)	$108,241
Profit from Ownership	($115,921)	$324,079
ROI (Return on Investment)	-58%	162%

---

93   Assumes Interest plus amortization.

94   Assumes property values increase at 3% annually.

This is a simple analysis that assumes interest plus amortization and property value increase at 3 percent annually. It's included to demonstrate the macro fundamentals of income property performance versus home ownership. Outcomes and numbers will vary depending on specific property circumstances, interest rates, geography, management skills, tax benefits, and a number of other considerations.

This may look good on paper, but not everyone can afford to purchase an apartment building or should. But if you can purchase a home, you can probably afford to purchase a triplex, duplex, or a home with an accessory dwelling unit (ADU). This allows you to live in one unit and rent out the others. The rent makes it a productive asset, and that income you're generating helps you pay off your mortgage while the home grows in value over time.

Warren Buffett has frequently spoken about the power of productive assets. Stocks, bonds, real estate, and even farmland fit this category because they produce income over time. What doesn't? Assets like gold and cryptocurrency. You can only sell those assets for what someone else is willing to pay. They don't generate profit or pay any interest. Buffett famously said that he wouldn't buy all the Bitcoin in the world for $25 but would immediately purchase a 1 percent interest in all the farmland in the United States for $25 billion.[95] He couldn't do anything with the Bitcoin; he'd have to sell it back to earn a profit. But that farmland is going to produce food for years to come. Productive assets are not only the investments with the highest returns, but they are also the safest.

---

95 Jing Pan, "Warren Buffett Says He Doesn't Own Bitcoin Because 'It Isn't Going to Do Anything'—He'd Rather Own These 2 Highly Productive Assets Instead," Yahoo, February 13, 2023, https://www.yahoo.com/now/warren-buffett-just-said-doesn-220000034.html.

That doesn't mean that Bitcoin and gold don't have their place in an investment portfolio, because they do for some people. However, most people purchase assets like gold out of fear. The opposite is also true, and it doesn't mean you're safe if you only select stocks and bonds. You need to pick the right stock in the right sector and ensure you're not paying too much in fees, but if you can find the right productive asset, that investment will always outperform a nonproductive asset over time.

By investing in productive assets over nonproductive assets, you can increase your capital by three, four, or five times. It goes back to what we discussed earlier about diversification and discipline.

This still doesn't address how to approach home buying. For many, this will be the biggest purchase of their lives, and it can make or break their financial future. That's why a house should not be your first investment, but your fourth or fifth, after accumulating a portfolio that includes tax-advantaged retirement funds and index funds. And you don't want to purchase a home until you have a second source of passive income. As Warren Buffett says, "Never depend on a single income. Make an investment to create a second source." He even goes so far as to say that if you haven't created a second source of income by the age of forty-five, you've done yourself a disservice.

> **If you can find the right productive asset, that investment will always outperform a nonproductive asset over time.**

PROTECTING YOUR WEALTH

Debt, deficits, and the Great Conflux will have the most detrimental impact on those with money, so if you've built wealth, you must protect it. We have no way of knowing when this crisis will occur and how it will materialize, so you want to plan for all possibilities. Here are ways you can insulate yourself and your money.

Don't Keep All Your Money in the United States

One result of the Great Conflux could be the collapse of the dollar and hyperinflation, which would lead to a fiscal crisis in the United States. If that happens, you don't want all your assets in the United States or tied to US-related investments. Diversification is something that the wealthy need to do more broadly, both in and out of the country.

Survivorship Life Insurance

As this crisis unfolds, Congress will likely increase inheritance taxes to bridge the debt. That will burden the wealthy, but you can plan for that through insurance policies, specifically a joint survivorship policy, also known as a second-to-die policy.

This joint life insurance policy, typically held by a husband and wife, will pay out the benefit to the next generation (typically the children) when both parties have passed away. Since the life expectancy of two people is longer than one, and insurance companies can collect premium payments for a longer period before paying out the benefit, this policy is less expensive than a policy for a single person.

The beneficiaries of survivorship life insurance receive a higher cash payout that is tax-free. More significantly, it's an excellent way to help the next generation pay hefty estate and inheritance taxes, especially if there is little liquidity in the estate.

Capital Gains versus Ordinary Income

When you sell assets at a higher price than what you purchased them for, that profit is referred to as a capital gain. Capital gains are subject to taxes, but the long-term capital gains tax rate is roughly 15 to 20 percent. Compared to the 45 percent tax rate that those earning wages in a high bracket are forced to pay, it's in your best interest to receive the bulk of your money through capital gains and not ordinary income. That's another reason productive assets are beneficial and the best way to build and maintain wealth.

Opportunity Zones

In 2017, the government attempted to spur economic development in certain distressed areas labeled as opportunity zones by offering significant tax breaks to those investing in commercial real estate and businesses in those communities. The investment needs to be made through a qualified opportunity fund (QOF), which makes over 90 percent of its investments in these zones to qualify.

This is similar to a 1031 exchange, only the original investment isn't limited to real estate profit. Any capital gain can qualify, and it helps you protect your money from capital gain tax. However, this is a deferral and a reduction of tax.

If your investment is held for five years, the amount you're taxed on decreases by 10 percent. For example, if you invest $100,000, you're only taxed on $90,000. Hold the investment for seven years and only $85,000 is subject to capital gains tax. Meanwhile, your investment grows tax-free, and if you hold it for ten years or more, you still have to pay tax on the $85,000, but you won't have to pay taxes on any additional profit when you sell.

This is a win-win. Investing in opportunity zones lets you do good by contributing to communities in need while also lowering your taxes and increasing your returns.

GETTING YOUR KIDS OFF ON THE RIGHT FOOT

If you're a parent, it's your responsibility to provide for your children, and part of that involves giving them the tools required to become financially stable. That doesn't mean making everything easy for them and fulfilling their every need—just the opposite. It means helping them come to these realizations on their own, so they can create healthy habits for life. You know what's best for your family, and every family situation is different, so what works for you might not work for someone else. Here are a few simple ways to build that foundation to help secure your children's financial future.

Educational 529 Account

This journey starts right when your children are born. With a name and a social security number, you can open an educational 529 account for your child. This is an excellent way for parents and grandparents to put away money for their children and grow their earnings tax-free. This can help you save for college and even primary and secondary schools. The specifics of these accounts differ per state, and you can withdraw the money at any time as long as you spend it on qualified education expenses, such as tuition, room and board, and computers.

The Benefits of Hard Work

Instilling the habit of hard work in your children is a skill that will pay dividends throughout their lives. There is no substitute for hard work, so encourage your child to work for an allowance. When they get older and reach high school, encourage them to get a summer job. It doesn't need to be a full-time job or get in the way of anything else they might want to do. The goal is for them to understand the nature of work and develop an appreciation for money.

Savings Accounts

When your kids start making money, create a savings account and help them develop the habit of putting 20 percent away into that account. It doesn't matter if that money isn't a significant amount. The goal is to establish a healthy habit. The reason many adults have money problems is not because they don't make enough money; it's because they never learned the importance of saving their money.

Spending Strategies

Teaching kids to live within their means and not spend money on things they don't need can be difficult. Delayed gratification and understanding the benefit of putting off what you want today, so you can have more of what you need tomorrow, is something few adults appreciate. But many of these steps are connected and feed off each other. As soon as your kids begin working and trade their time for money, they will be less likely to throw it away on worthless consumer goods, and if they've already developed the habit of saving 20 percent of what they earn, it will be hardwired into them as they get older.

Build Credit

You don't want to tempt your kids at a young age by giving them a credit card before they're ready to use it responsibly, but there are other ways you can help them build credit. You can make them authorized users on your cards without giving them access to the card or even knowing about the account. Good credit can go extremely far in helping your children secure student loans, land a job during college, and eventually rent their first apartment.

Investing Early

In addition to opening an educational 529 plan, my wife and I created 401(k) accounts for our kids when they were young. As soon as they started making money, we encouraged them to take some of that money they saved and transfer it into their 401(k) account every month. Getting kids to appreciate the benefits of saving can be difficult, but if you teach them about compounding and show them how their online account is growing over time, it can be a powerful visual that makes the point for you.

* * *

Kids aren't taught financial literacy in school. They aren't taught how to save and invest their money, so it's easy for them to develop bad habits when left to their own devices. If they don't have to work and earn money, it will be much more difficult for them to appreciate the value of a dollar. Instilling healthy financial habits in your children at a young age is one of the greatest gifts you can give them because it will set them up for future success like little else will.

KEY TAKEAWAYS

- Investing is not gambling. You need to make informed and educated decisions to lower risk and maximize your reward.
- Remember the five fundamental principles of investing:

1. Compounding: Einstein referred to compounding as the eighth wonder of the world, and it comes down to earning interest on top of your interest.
2. Diversification: Don't put all your eggs in one basket. Investing is cyclical, and you never want more than 10 percent of your capital in a single investment.
3. Consistency: Work hard, save, invest, and repeat.
4. Using the government: You can use the government printing press to your advantage by investing stimulus money and using entities like the Small Business Association to get your business off the ground.
5. Patience: Nothing happens overnight. This is a long game.

- Mutual funds are moronic. When getting started, take advantage of these investment vehicles to minimize your risk, maximize your return, and build wealth over the long term:

  - 401(k)
  - Traditional IRA
  - Roth IRA
  - Index funds

- Tap into the power of productive assets, such as real estate, that generate a second source of income.
- Once you've built your wealth, protect it through diversification, survivorship life insurance, capital gains, and opportunity zones.
- If you're a parent, get your children off on the right foot by instilling healthy financial habits at a young age.

EPILOGUE

The Power of the Human Spirit and Technology

The atomic bomb proved that fusion was possible. It's a reaction that puts out more energy than it takes in, and it's the same type of energy-producing reaction that powers the sun. What had not been possible for the past sixty years was controlling and harnessing that type of energy and using it to our advantage. That changed in December 2022, when the National Ignition Facility in California proved that harnessing fusion power is possible.

This discovery can potentially change life as we know it by creating an endless, carbon-free energy source. That would solve countless energy, climate, and financial problems, but we have a long way to go before we get to that point. Many challenges loom on the horizon, but it's just one of the latest examples of the power of human ingenuity.

Look at what the human race has accomplished in the past one hundred years. Technology hasn't grown linearly—it's compounded. A computer that once took up an entire room fifty years ago can now fit inside the phone we carry in our pockets. During that period, GPS technology went from only being available to the military and the airlines to becoming standard with every one of those phones. There are advances in quantum computing and artificial intelligence that will create remarkable opportunities and advances, but that's only the beginning.

Throughout history, we've done things that people never thought were possible. From the first man-made flight to putting a man on the moon, history is filled with examples of monumental achievements that changed the world and redefined what we knew was possible. While humans may exhibit moronic behavior, we also know how to thrive during a crisis. It's how we've survived as a species for so long. When faced with problems for which we don't have good solutions, we're forced to get creative. We adapt, transform, and emerge more resilient and resourceful.

This belief is at the core of those leading the longevity companies we discussed in chapter 1 that are quickly making extended life spans a reality. Joe Percoco, cofounder and co-CEO of fintech startup Titan, sees an opportunity in such moments: "You actually need a disorienting event to build something transcendental."[96] It's difficult to imagine all the innovations that await us and what problems they might solve.

I am a true believer. I believe in the human spirit's ability to triumph during times of crisis. I believe in the human ability to innovate when necessary to solve catastrophic problems, and I believe that the United States is leading that charge. By living here, I have more opportunities than most other people around the world. I am beyond grateful to have been given the gift of living and raising my family in the United States. I owe a debt of gratitude to my country

---

96 James Vincent, "5 Timeless Lessons about Innovation from Some of the Most Successful Founders," Fast Company, October 19, 2022, https://www.fastcompany.com/90796700/5-timeless-lessons-about-innovation-from-some-of-the-most-successful-founders.

The Power of the Human Spirit and Technology

for the freedoms it provides and the prosperity it paves the way for. There is no doubt that part of my success can be attributed to the incredible opportunities the United States has provided. If I were born in another part of the world that didn't have all the same benefits, I would not be as successful, free, and secure as I am today.

Despite all our problems, I feel truly blessed, and I have great hope for our future. The world and humanity are better today by almost every measurable metric, and I believe that trend will continue, so the future will be even better. The power of people, purpose, and community is a force that will continue to change and improve the world. The opportunity is there for you to be a part of that; you need to take that opportunity and not let it pass you by.